Thinking Hats and Coloured Turbans

Kirpal Singh

PEARSON
Prentice
Hall

Singapore   London   New York   Toronto   Sydney   Tokyo   Madrid
Mexico City   Munich   Paris   Capetown   Hong Kong   Montreal

Published in 2004 by
Prentice Hall
Pearson Education South Asia Pte Ltd
23/25 First Lok Yang Road, Jurong
Singapore 629733

Pearson Education offices in Asia: *Bangkok, Beijing, Hong Kong, Jakarta, Kuala Lumpur, Manila, New Delhi, Seoul, Singapore, Taipei, Tokyo, Shanghai*

Printed in Singapore

4   3   2   1
07   06   05   04

ISBN 013-102-533-3

For

JWEE

eh, bagerok

-and-

for Ann Medlock-

creative genius-

with love

[signature]

Feb '10

CONTENTS

ACKNOWLEDGEMENTS

God is great! In my life I've been very blessed by being able to meet and converse with some of the brightest and best of our times. In the writing of this book, I have, I am definite, been influenced by all I have met, known and talked to. Like the Tennysonian hero here alluded to my experience has been rich, complex, perplexing and manifold. Creativity, matters creative, have always been very close to my heart. So when I name specific individuals, my first acknowledgement must go out to all who will remain anonymous because they were there just when I needed them. To all of these tremendous individuals, please accept my gratitude; remember, without you this would have been a very different undertaking.

I must place on record my thanks to the Wharton-SMU Research Centre for giving me a research grant which enabled me to travel and meet so many of the wonderful people discussed, cited and mentioned in this book. In particular I want to thank Professor Tsui Kai Chong (former Dean of the School of Business at Singapore Management University) and Professor Roberto Mariano, current Chair of the Research Committee. It is necessary that researchers be given considerable latitude so that their attention is concentrated on their research rather than the nitty-gritty details of how every dollar is spent. In this regard the ever-excellent Priscilla Cheng of the Research Centre has always been at hand to help me: thank you, Priscilla. My Provost, the inimitable Prof Tan Chin Tiong, has been a pillar of support and encouragement. I want to thank him particularly for his help in going through Appendix IV.

Ms Gillian Chee, formerly of Pearson Education South Asia, first suggested that I offer my book for publication. Under her gentle persuasion I agreed. But I have to thank Mr Chua Hong Koon, the Publishing Director and Ms Joanne Tan, the Managing Editor, for the great job they did with the process of bringing the book out. Joanne, in particular, has been especially scrupulous in making sure mistakes are minimal. Joanne is a terrific personality and no author could have wished for a better, enlightened editor! A special word of thanks must go to Ms Pauline Chua and Ms Angela Chew for their cooperation and support while they were helping me with the book. As they say, having the help of good people when it comes to publishing is essential – I have been very lucky.

Though this might sound like nepotism, I must thank my three beautiful – and highly creative – daughters Sarah, Areta and Misha. Without their constant egging on and challenging (and sharing of their own achievements), again, this would have been a more diminished book. To Clarinda my wife, who has been a source of inspiration and delight for these many years, I can only say here, "Hey, we made it!"

Many of my colleagues at the university and elsewhere have helped me in many big and small ways. Most of them are mentioned in the book but I must thank the following by name because they went out of their way to critique different chapters/parts and in so doing made me rethink and rephrase many pages: My colleagues, Professors Dawn Dekle, Oscar Hauptman and Leong Kwong Sin (Singapore Management University), Bernhardt Trout (Massachusetts Institute of Technology), Peter Nazareth (University of Iowa), Dennis Haskell (University of Western Australia) and Syd Harrex (Flinders University). There are too many others to name here, people who were so kind as to read fragments of the book and give me valuable (and often insightful) feedback: to all of these lovely individuals I say, Thank you.

I must thank the seven highly creative and fascinating characters who fill the case histories – each of their individual narratives is a high watermark of achievement and I do want to take this opportunity to say, "Hey good people, thank you and may the Lord bless you, always!" To the many different persons from whom I gained interesting insights and have quoted many a time, my deep gratitude.

What can I honestly say to the very nice people who have endorsed my book and given me such glowing recommendations? Well, let me be creative and say, "Anytime I can use one of the many folds of my turbans to buy you guys dinner, let me know!"

Finally, if I have inadvertently offended anyone, I ask for your indulgence. It is hard to write a book on this subject without feelings, strong feelings!

Kirpal Singh
September, 2003

PREFACE

It must be made **absolutely** clear right now that this book is primarily **exploratory** – it does not pretend to stake proven and scientifically 100% correct claims to **any** thing. What it does do, however, is to offer insights, challenges and, most significantly, narratives – stories, anecdotes, examples, cases – the things, they say, which make up the **creative** impulse, the creative moment.

I make no apologies for the way this book is written and laid out. I make no apologies, particularly, for its *tone*, its conversational *style* and, most of all, its often *irreverent* references, asides and digs. No book on and about **creativity** can be written to satisfy *existing* standards of scholastic demand and expectations. By its very nature, almost as if by definition, creativity insists and exists by its **difference**. Hence this book is going to prove different, even upsetting, for those who have picked it up expecting another treatise on this complicated subject. Should you, my dear reader, be one such, you are perfectly at liberty to put it down and walk away, pretending nothing happened; no one needs to know, no one will know (if you are clever enough!) that you fall into that category of people who reach out to things wanting change, but withdraw the moment they are challenged. Yes, this book is going to challenge all readers. And I make no apologies for this either.

From time immemorial countless accounts, descriptions and treatises have been written about this strange and fascinatingly haunting topic known to us as creativity. Religious pundits and their polarized colleagues, the atheists, have all discussed and debated the nature of creativity. No consensus, as far as I know, has ever been reached. Again, I make no apologies for the fact that this book will not yield any consensus; it will not **define** creativity for you. This is **not** a book which will whet your appetite for **knowing** creativity. No.

So, then, what **is** this book about?

Well, it **is** about creativity. It is about men and women who have proven creative. It is about the ways in which we have attempted (albeit mainly in vain) to come to terms with this primal source of all we see, feel, taste, touch, hear and sense. It deals with one of the most elusive of all human experiences. It explores and attempts to tell a story and take the reader on a journey. It is not a journey on a roller-coaster (even though it might feel like one sometimes!), nor is it a journey on a slow paddleboat (no matter how charming and quaint such a ride might be). Is it therefore a balance between a roller-coaster and a paddleboat? No. Anyone engaged with what may even remotely be pegged under the label creativity cannot be balanced. So is this in itself a contention? Yes and no. Creativity is rarely about balancing, though a good balancing act can be highly creative.

Get the drift? I shall not invoke Wordsworth ("*My drift, I fear, is obvious* ...") here for the evident reason that non-literary readers might accuse me of being trapped, like many writers before me who have tried to wrestle with creativity, in the world of literary nuances and allusions. But, yes, creativity **is** nuancy and yes, it is frequently better understood through allusion.

And both nuance and allusion here start with the title of the book itself. I am not merely trying to be clever, funny or cheeky by using the well-worn term which a previous guru of creative thinking has made so popular that many believe the phrase belongs to him exclusively; nor am I dismissing the more interestingly engaging elements present through such a belief! And if you are wondering how, where and why the turbans come in (and I was told the other day that in some parts of the world people who wear turbans are now also known as **towelheads** – quite a creative and ingenious formulation, don't you think?), let me reassure you it is not simply on account of the fact that I wear a turban.

I have read and been taken in by the work of de Bono, as I have been by reading the profound works of many other writers in the field. Throughout this book I have desisted quoting any one of them, though they have all influenced me tremendously. Am I being intellectually shy? Not at all. I acknowledge **all** their impact on my own ruminations and excursions into this vast field of human endeavour. I doubt if any one of us can lay claim to exclusivity. Like beauty, which is there for all of us to behold and enjoy, so, too, is creativity there for all of us to reckon with and try to fathom.

Thinking Hats and Coloured Turbans didn't just come about out of the blue. It came about when one fine day a visitor to Singapore dropped by my university, asked to sit in and observe my class on Creative Thinking and during the break said, "So you must use quite a bit of de Bono's **thinking hats**?" I answered, "No, I use a lot of my own **coloured turbans**." He looked at me in total disbelief before bursting out in laughter. We both laughed. That was good. Very good. I have often looked back at that moment as being "special" and I hope when he (Joop Verloop) reads this book he will know that if other circumstances had been right he, too, would have been more directly a part of this journey.

That first part of the title and my engagement with Joop Verloop naturally led to the second part: creativity across cultures. With the new millennium came, for me, not only a new world order in the sphere of economics and politics, but more fundamentally, also, in the ways with which we think about such a basic concept as creativity. Indeed, both Joop and I saw creativity very differently; we understood the term differently; we discoursed on it differently. Was this simply because his first language was Dutch while mine was English (or as he thought, Punjabi)? No. It dawned on me, very quickly, that at heart we were responding from what theorists would know as **deep structure**. Embedded (what a word, how creatively - with all the ironies known to those of us who make it our business to know words - it has been used in the Iraq War!) as it was deep in each of our consciousness, creativity spelt different things to Joop and to me.

Thus began my own journey. Starting slowly, it picked up momentum, encouraged by my own experience of teaching Creative Thinking at the Singapore Management University where Creative Thinking (CT as it is affectionately called by my bosses and students) is a core university module. In Appendix IV I describe, in a much abbreviated fashion, what I do in these CT sessions. I should caution you, dear reader, that like the many students who have been through this course, you may find yourself immersed in it more than you might at first think – any exciting encounter or experience of creativity is bound to have a lasting impact.

For creativity is in itself a temptation. And I state this with love and respect. Because when we lose love and respect for temptation we lose something quintessential; we lose the capacity for wonder! Someone advised us a long time ago that "a man's reach must exceed his grasp" and it is in such an advice that the seeds of creativity are to be found. The Adam and Eve story thus becomes a great **creativity** myth, in addition to being just a **creation** myth. And through the centuries theologians, thinkers, philosophers and poets have actively enlarged our limited understanding of temptation through their several discourses on this knotty subject. If there were no temptation there would be nothing. But this also becomes problematized by the agonizing anguish of a man like Shakespeare's Lear ("Nothing will come out of nothing. Speak again").

Wonder makes us enter those mysterious and unchartered territories, both imagined and real, which lie before us like that first temptation. Creativity, I have found through long, hard research and practice, is not for the weak; it is not for those who are afraid of the unknown. No. Creativity belongs to those whose fortune it is to be marked; designated carriers of a thirst and a hunger not easily fulfilled.

This small book is thus a tribute to creativity and to those who manifest it. We are all blessed because some among us have had it within them to confront temptation – and trace all the subsequent stages of their entrapment. For those who are creative, temptation is not a bad word or an experience to be shunned. No; on the contrary, temptation beckons the creative mind and as it wanders through the hazy maze of its own making, creativity both rewards and punishes. I know, for I have experienced both.

It is important that you, my dear reader, travel with me in faith and with faith. Ours is not an age of belief but of mistrust and suspicion. I want you to move beyond our age, I want you to come with me and travel through this gentle journey of exploration. And after travelling, to share this with others, knowing that the arrival is only the culmination of an even more exciting process – the journey itself. To make our joint travelling both fun and challenging, I have departed from the "norm" in many ways – for example this book has four introductions instead of the customary one because I passionately believe that in discussing creativity, especially, there can never be just "one" thing, statement, example, affirmation. Creativity is **multiple**, multifarious; it comes in different forms, shapes, sizes, manifestations, testimonies, jokes, illustrations. So jump on, come travel with me.

Kirpal Singh

Introduction

Which came first, the fruit orange or the colour orange? When I was asked this question, I immediately replied "the fruit". But this also made me think of another well-known question: which comes first, the chicken or the egg?

From as far back as I can remember, I used to interject, to the annoyance of all those around, "Where does the rooster come in?" Because I figured, without the rooster, the chicken-and-egg thingy remains incomplete. It is amazing to note just how much time, energy and effort people spend, arguing, fighting, discussing, thinking and trying to figure out which came first – the chicken or the egg. And yet that crucial **other**, the rooster, seems to escape most people's notice.

Why does this happen? Why do we allow the most significant items to slip from our fingers and minds? Why do we respond in predictable ways? Why are we afraid of being provocative? Why? Why? Why?

Many years ago when I was teaching at the National University of Singapore I gave a lecture on my friend Arthur C. Clarke's insightful novel *Imperial Earth*. When the students' feedback came to me, I was quite astounded that many thought I was using a text which simply had no basis for its hypotheses! Comments such as **Kirpal Singh talks bull in class**; **Mr Singh ought to know his science better**; **Kirpal Singh should not talk about things which my religion objects to, etc, etc,** featured in the feedback. Why? Because I had lectured that, given Clarke's novel and the extrapolations it contained, one day soon we were bound to see cloning come about (I meant, of course, the cloning of humans!). Boy, was I attacked. Very luckily my Head and my Dean – a very interestingly creative individual himself – was compassionate and said, "Kirpal, I think it might be better for you to tone down your lectures a little … Even if you are right, this kind of feedback does you no good."

Precisely! Unintelligent, uninformed and worst of all, **anonymous** criticism given without the slightest consideration as to whether what the lecturer might have been saying had some merit does nothing but destroy the morale of most young university dons. I have had colleagues who have told me, again and again over the years, "It is no use fighting, the system will always win and will always find ways to make sure it is right." Yes, as does every being when attacked. We all fight for our survival and because we are supposed to be sentient beings, morally endowed, we rationalize our conduct. So, too, systems. Now at my present university I constantly urge my students to empower themselves by not hiding behind the veil of anonymity when giving feedback; what is the point when one is afraid to take ownership of the criticism or complaint one is making? More and more of my students, I am happy to state, are starting to do this. And this leads to a critical point about creativity.

I believe, fervently, that real creativity cannot and will not come about unless there is at least a modicum of **transparency**. Yes, there have been countless examples in tyrannical states, in communist nations, in dictatorships, to prove me wrong; yes, but we should also remember that in all of these instances, the **creative** element demonstrated itself **in spite** of the system, not **because** of it. And a nation, a culture, a community devoting itself to the making of a creative population, surely must understand this most basic of pronouncements: the more secretive one is, the more time it is going to take to nurture, sustain and nourish a genuinely creative or innovative culture.

I was reading a book about mind tools in which it was stated that it is necessary to sometimes ask truly provocative questions: for example, why must houses have roofs? By asking such seemingly silly and even stupid questions, the author argued, the mind is forced to think of reversals and alternatives. So we may come up with substitutes for roofs and this may lead to new products being offered in the market! Well, well, well. I guess I have always been provocative, right from the time when in the third year of elementary school I wore nine underpants to escape the pain of extreme caning. As it turned out, the nine underpants didn't help me because our smart teacher, noticing the bulk below my waist, made me take off *all* nine. Sometimes being creative, trying to outsmart the other, results in worse punishment. But I cannot but agree that asking awkward questions is a sure hallmark of the creative individual. This creature doesn't just sit there accepting all and absorbing all; what he does is raise challenging questions.

There was a teacher in an elementary school who always had a way of putting the pupils down. For example, in one lesson on the geography of the earth, she reeled off facts and figures about the oceans and the seas, the rivers and the mountains, etc. At the end of the lesson she asked if there were any questions. One small hand went up. "Yes, Teacher," said this shy little boy, "what is the weight of the earth?" Not knowing the answer, the teacher replied, "That is a very good question. Now boys and girls, I want you to go home and find out the correct answer; consider this your homework for today." Then she went straight to the library after school and noted the weight of the earth.

The next day the teacher came into class and asked, "So did any of you find the answer to the question 'What is the weight of the earth?'" Nobody raised his or her hand. "Well, I knew you lazy guys would not get the answer." Saying this, she triumphantly walked to the chalkboard and wrote a long set of numerals. "This," she said, gloatingly, "is the weight of the earth. Now, are there any more questions?" The same boy who had asked the first question put up his hand. "Teacher," he said calmly, "is that the weight of the earth with people on it or without people on it?" at which point the teacher, blushing red with ignorance, said, "Keep quiet and read your textbook."

The point of the story should be obvious. In our educational institutions are people who worry more about their own security than they do about the real pursuit of knowledge and understanding. Of course this is a sweeping generalization and of course there are good teachers who truly go out of their way to ensure that their students learn in the best possible way. But I am speaking of the majority of teachers. In my lifetime I have come across very few, very precious few, who have had the guts to admit to ignorance, to confess that their own education was, like most people's, limited. Why are we so afraid to admit ignorance? Is it shameful? Is it a real loss of face? Well, we had better reconsider what shame and losing face is because we are not going to get very far in creativity if we allow these unnecessary emotions to cripple our style.

You, dear reader, will probably have read many books dealing with this strange and indefinable thing called creativity. This book you are now reading is both about creativity and much that goes beyond it. Because that is what creativity is – it touches every aspect of our lives! My contention is that creativity, no matter how one tries to define it, explain it, explore it, state it and vilify it, cannot, and will never be, dissociated from the larger culture in which it finds itself. To talk about being creative minus those huge subsets of conditions, which invariably result in either encouraging or hindering creativity, is to be naive, to exist in a state in which somnambulism takes over from reason.

So this book is about many, many things. From upbringing to PhDs, from the general sensibilities of a people to the language(s) we speak, read and write. From pedagogies of learning and teaching to experiments in joking and working. By its very nature this book does not – and cannot – claim any finality: there are *no* final answers when we explore creativity. There cannot be. What we have, in the end, is at best a clearer awareness of the multitudinous complexity surrounding this vexing topic. Have we ever understood why God created Man? Indeed, when asked who He was, God merely responded, "I am who I am." Creativity does not offer scholars the consolation of a QED. Creativity is not a triumph; it is a promise. It is not the pot of gold at the end of the rainbow; rather, it is perhaps its many inviting colours. Creativity teases; it makes us uneasy about things, about people, about ideas, about life and living, about our systems, our institutions, our bosses and our colleagues, our friends, lovers, spouses, parents, siblings, children – about literally everything. And yet it eludes fixing. Creativity is *not* a problem which can be quick-fixed. It cannot even be slow-fixed. Creativity is a **state of being**, a state of realization that deep within us are immense possibilities for finding out new ways of doing things, new ways of being, new ways of co-relating, new connections, relationships, services, products and ideas. Creativity is *not* a problem waiting to be solved, but a **solution** waiting to be used, processed and learnt.

Am I being honest in saying I learnt much from this book or that book? Not really, because what I have to say here comes from more than 45 years of **conscious** living, of being alive to my environment and to the many delights and punishments it has put in my way. I am a very blessed human being: I come from mixed parentage; my children are also of mixed parentage. I grew up in four different countries: Singapore, where I was born, Malaysia (then Federation of Malaya), where I spent the first six years of my life; India, which was the country that most informed my paternal grandmother who brought me up, and Scotland, from whose distant shores my mother travelled to the exotic east and fell hopelessly in love with a tall, handsome boxer who trounced his opponent with just one left hook while she, my mother, sat and watched from the ringside. How do I explain the crosscurrents of my own thinking? I will not even attempt to do so because I can't – and because it is useless to try and map the subtle maturing of mindscape which has been both traumatized by life as well as blessed in the most extraordinary of ways. When I was very young my grandmother used to cradle me in her arms and tell me stories about warriors, who are now stars in the night sky, and weird animals who kept vigilance over me as I lay asleep. As a writer, especially as a poet, I am still trying to fathom the fullness of metaphor – that powerful organizing human symbol whose business it is to tease us out of our complacencies. Are we still solving the puzzle about the serpent's temptation of Eve? Would we not agree that this great myth is one of the finest examples of the human creative spirit at work in strong metaphoric language?

Because of my sustained study of literature, particularly English Literature, I am frequently asked to give lectures on English Language, English Literature or just about anything which touches on these interesting subjects. I often quote these famous lines from Robert Burns:

> My love's like a red, red rose
> That's newly sprung in May

Most of my listeners, especially these days, have never heard of Burns so I tell them this was the same fellow who wrote *Auld Lang Syne* ("Ahhh," I hear them sigh). I continue, "Look at just that fantastic first line, *My love's like a red, red rose*. What do we make of it?" Time passes and my respondents suggest several different readings of this line. But none, literally none till now, has ever said anything like the following: "It is necessary to note that real roses always have thorns; therefore Burns in one remarkable line has summed up the glory and the tragedy of love: it both gives life and kills." On a lighter note, many of us know the nursery rhyme, *Jack and Jill went up the hill/To fetch a pail of water/Jack fell down and broke his crown/and Jill came tumbling after.* Yes. But few, so precious few, ever ask the question, "Why did Jack and Jill have to go *up* a hill to fetch water?"

I am being serious, like the clowns of yore. We remember that jesters were so designated that their freedom to question the monarch was a guarantee. I sometimes ruefully wonder whether in losing the great tradition of jesters we have also lost the capacity for creative thinking. Jesters, jokers, men and women who almost always have a way of **twisting** what is said or heard – these are very special people with very special gifts. They show us how we may look at the world with original, fresh eyes and in so doing, maybe, just maybe, still retain our sanity.

For in a world becoming so manifestly silly where people risk their lives for **embedded truths**, where the grooming of a cocker spaniel is more vital than feeding a six-month-old baby, where the wild ecstasy of scoring 100% over a machine is more orgasmic than the orgasms realized during sex, where the saving of one's face is more important than the truth which is being shared – in such a crazy world we need creativity and we need creative people. It is no longer enough to say we have all the paraphernalia to bring creativity about; what is wanted is the nerve to truly bring it about. Too much talk with empty delivery has resulted in the impoverished condition we are in today; all over the world people are crying out for creative solutions to their problems, for creativity to bring new meaning to the lives of men and women lost in the bewilderment of a confusing humanity.

This book does not promise immediate results. No. But it guarantees engagement; it guarantees challenge; it guarantees provocation. While reading this book is not going to make you an instant creator, it *is* going to dig out and dig up your own deeply embedded creative self. For we all have one. This is the way we were made.

This is not a scholarly book in the usual sense of the word. It is not meant to be one. Indeed, scholarship can be said to be opposed to creativity because creativity deals with the unborn; scholarship merely probes the **already**. Throughout there will be repetitions, there will be gross statements, general thrusts of intellect with no undertow, crude simplifications (how simple the act of sex, how complex the result!), broad demonstrations and amplifications – all with a view to impress upon you, the reader, just what a journey the voyage of creativity entails. Are you ready for it? Truly ready? Here is an exercise, which should tell you whether you are ready to embark on this journey.

Sit comfortably. Anywhere. Take a few deep breaths to relax. Gently close your eyes. Travel to where you feel totally at ease with the world, at ease with your Self. Enjoy the space. Think of love. Think of the one person with whom you have not made love for a long, long time. Think of that one person for whom you haven't even had time. This is you. Your Self. Think. Make love to your Self. Ask forgiveness from your Self because you have neglected it for so long. Being forgiven, ask for blessings. Blessed, be happy. Luxuriate in this newfound joy. Now, gently, come back to where you are. Slowly open your eyes. Are you ready?

Introduction 2

So you enter a lift and you see two others already in it. First scenario: You look at the two and then with your head down, press the lift button and wait. Second scenario: You see the two in the lift, smile at them and say, "Hello, good morning, how are you today?" They smile back. You press the lift button and wait. Third scenario: You catch the eyes of the two and say to them, "You know, guys, I have been thinking. We often see each other in this lift yet we don't know one another. How about you guys coming round to my house for dinner tomorrow as it is Saturday?"

Which scenario, dear reader, would you say represents creativity?

Here is a simple story. Pay careful attention to it.

The chief of prisons wrote to the superintendents of the various prisons in the country to say that the cost of bullets was so high that something had to be done before the Prisons Department went seriously into the red. The superintendents upon receiving this memo started thinking about what to do. One clever superintendent thought of something creative and proceeded to invite the chief to his prison so the chief could see how his prison was reducing bullet costs.

On the appointed day, the superintendent proudly said, "Sir, do you know the reason for the cost of bullets being so high? Lately we have had to execute many prisoners, and so many rounds of bullets have had to be used. However, Sir, I have come up with a creative idea which will put an effective end to any bullet use."

"Wow!" said the chief. "You must truly have an original idea for this."

"Yes, Sir," said the superintendent, with a beaming smile on his face. "I have instructed my Death Squad to tie the condemned prisoner to the back of a jeep and drag him round and round the prison square until he dies. In this way not a single bullet is used."

Not wanting to discourage him, the chief smiled at this and said, "Yes, not a single bullet being used means bullet expenses will really be reduced in this prison."

"Yes, Sir," said the superintendent.

"But," pointed out the chief, "you won't save much on gas, will you?"

Here is another anecdote. It is written by the famous French writer, Jean-Paul Sartre, and is paraphrased here. What does it tell us about **creativity**?

In a very neat and tidy house near Bushnell in mid-west America, a conscientious mother explained to her five-year-old son the mysteries of life and death.

"As the Bible tells us," she said, "we are nothing but dust. Dust unto dust. When you are older, Tom, you will know more about this. For now, remember, birth and death, life, is nothing but dust."

Tom, the son, noted this and went on with his daily routine. One day a toy car he was playing with disappeared under his bed. To retrieve it, Tom went under the bed, lifted the overhanging sheets and, lo and behold, there was a heap of dust gathered there!

"Mum! Mum!" Tom called out loudly. "Quick, come here! There's someone being born or dying right here, under my bed!"

By now it should be pretty obvious that it is very, very hard to decide on and draw a clear line distinguishing between creative and non-creative. And yet, no one reading this will say, "Therefore, creativity is nonsense." Why?

From time immemorial, human beings, animals, even plants, have had to be creative to survive. Given its biology, each species had to find a way of dealing with the environment to stay alive and perpetuate its kind. Some huge and powerful myths have gathered around early survival stories. The story of the discovery of fire is but one. Some of us may recall that Sisyphus was punished by Zeus for giving the gift of fire to humans. Symbolically, this signalled the arrival of Knowledge among men. Metaphorically, it conveyed the sense of warmth. Literally, it meant that with fire, men and women could keep themselves warm and also – creatively – use fire as a weapon to keep enemies at bay. Though hundreds of thousands of years have passed since the first recorded use of fire, this special element still remains a major threat as well as a major ally. As we say, fire is a good servant but a very bad master!

Is there a lesson here for us who want to explore the nature of creativity? Is creativity as dangerous as fire and thus to be closely watched and guarded? Is there always some punishment meted out to those who bring about creative designs, plans, events or ideas? Should we reward our creative types? How do we reward them? More and more questions. By now it will be abundantly clear that any discussion or exploration of creativity is bound to be complex, complicated, and almost without consensus.

Someone said, "For many, when opportunity knocks, it is noise."

Just reflect, for a moment, on this blunt but apt statement. Yes, for many people all over the world, opportunity knocking on their door is a nuisance, an intrusion into their world of calm and quiet, an unwelcome visitor to their comfort zone. Why? Because if we listened to opportunity's knocking and opened the door for it to come into our lives we would start doing things differently and bring about change. For most people this is not **on**! Change, the one constant perhaps in most humans' existence, is anathema, a threat, a daunting prospect which brings more anxiety than assurance. Most of us fear change because we don't know what it will bring in its wake. Change is risk. And risk is not worth taking unless the end results are very clear.

And yet without change we wouldn't be where we are today. For all of us the moment of change, that rare glimpse of opportunity, the shimmering vista of the future, is a delicate option. It demands that we make choices, and in making a choice, embrace all that it entails. How often have we made statements such as "If I had only known that this would be the result, I would not have done it."? Or "Maybe she will change her mind since I have opted to marry her."? Or "If only the weather remains like today's for the next three months, my method of harvesting will prove the best."? Many individuals hesitate and hang on the moments of opportunity, not knowing what to do. Like T. S. Eliot's Prufrock, many remain obsessed or preoccupied with that anxious second of apprehension and decision-making, rather than forge ahead, grasping risk and chance in both their hands!

Most of us are creatures of habit. We like the way we are. We seek ways and means of improving ourselves, of making more money, of trying to become more powerful, etc. All these ways and means however, are usually within given and quite fixed boundaries. For centuries we have been conditioned to be normal and thus not rock any boat! Rocking boats is a terrible pastime, most people will advise us, because, they say, in rocking boats, innocent people might get hurt by the giddy rhythms of the new rocking which their constitutions are not familiar with. In other words, change will come about and their whole metabolism will be disturbed, or more correctly, undermined.

Recall the scenario of entering the lift and encountering two people in it. In the first scenario, the most commonly observed, everyone is comfortable because nothing is said or done that is even slightly out of the ordinary. In the second scenario, the two already in the lift are engaged momentarily in conversation but then are left with nothing to think about or do. It is the third scenario where any semblance of **real** change is present: You want to have the two over for dinner! Wow! This is a far cry from Scenarios 1 and 2, and will therefore entail a ritual of verbal – sometimes gesticural – responses. The lives of the two will never be the same again, whether or not they actually take up the dinner invitation. Something momentous has taken place, making the worlds of these two human beings markedly different and giving them a totally new, unexpected perspective on fellow lift-passengers! Notice that we are talking about **normal** situations because in **unusual** situations, such as, say, a lift breakdown, intercourse among lift passengers takes place because of fear. Being trapped, or at least caught in the same unhappy and unwanted condition (very few people would want the lifts they are riding in to break down!), the passengers seek solace and comfort through interaction.

Whatever else we may say or think or feel about creativity, one thing is immediately obvious – creativity brings about change. About this there cannot be any rational dispute.

Yes, some of us might say, chuckling about the fact that in the illustration about bullets and gas, while there was change, it was a funny sort of change which in itself resulted in even higher expenses! Creativity in itself is seldom concerned about good or bad change, but just pure, essential change. Quintessentially, creativity and change go hand in hand, perhaps not always with the same rhythm, but certainly with the same gravity, bringing about that which previously did not exist or matter. God is recognized to be the greatest Creator of all because He brought about the biggest change of all time – He created everything! Do all creators, therefore, become like God? Do creative people imbibe of God-sense/God-essence? An excruciating question, asked by philosophers from the time humans began to think (Question: Did we begin by thinking? **I think therefore I am**. I don't think and therefore I am not!). A friend said to me, "You know, Kirpal, judging by the way some of these so-called creative-types behave, one would imagine they are all gods." I laughed when I heard this. I laughed because, yes, creativity *does* encourage a small bit of arrogance in most of us and, yes, I know only too well that many people assume an air of arrogance when they believe they are creative.

So what can we say or do about little Tom and his well-intentioned mum? Well, we might say Tom's mother was trying to be creative in trying to explain to her small son the mysteries of life and death. It is hard enough to talk to these young blighters about the birds and the bees, what more about life and death! Was the mother, though, being truly creative? She was also connecting Tom's queries about life and death to her Book of Faith. Was she both creative and non-creative? I will let you figure this one out. For me the most creative thing about this story is the creativity in the anecdote!

Creativity = Change + ...

Here is another exercise. Make yourself comfortable, preferably by sitting on the floor. Taking well-paced deep breaths, gently close your eyes and clear your mind of "overload", that is, any ideas, images and thoughts which clutter the mind and hinder the process of clear thinking. After a few minutes of doing this, focus on your life and choose two significant events or people who have brought change to your life. Think about each of these for about three minutes. When you have focused clearly on both, gently bring yourself to the present and ask, "Where am I now in relation to these changes?"

I have always believed that there are as many definitions of creativity as there are human beings. Most of us think we know what creativity is, namely, what it is all about and what it entails. Nevertheless there are bewildering issues and questions which pop up the moment we actually try our hand at defining this term. Countless scholars and theorists have done so, each finally confirming that here is an elusive term which cannot be given any universal definition or formula. Creativity is not mathematics, not chemistry, not biology, not philosophy, not art, not language, not culture, not education, not any one thing! It is *all* of these and more. This is what makes it so fascinatingly challenging. Until a few years ago I was happy to be a scholar, specializing in the literature of the post-colonial world, and of course, irritating many of the old guard in traditional English Literature circles by raising and asking irritating questions like, "Well, in Pope's *Rape of the Lock*, surely the ending of Canto IV suggests that Belinda would have loved to be actually 'raped' rather than just have her hair cut!" Or, more surely, Lady Macbeth's problem vis-à-vis her husband is that while she acts under the influence of alcohol, he doesn't and so on and so forth. I remember my university teachers used to throw up their hands in despair sometimes at the many nuisance-questions (as one of them put it) that I used to raise during tutorials. (Question: Is the traditional method of teaching at universities – a mass lecture with small-group tutorials – still appropriate? Does this pedagogic mode offer creativity room to manoeuvre?)

Well, time has moved on and so have I. For the past six years or so I have become increasingly keen to know how creativity functions; for example, how certain individuals tend to be more creative than others, how indeed certain cultures, nations and civilizations tended to be more creative throughout history, and how and why creativity can be promoted to be the vital ingredient for survival in this third millennium.

One answer to the question why some nations, some communities, some cultures and some individuals seem to be more creative than others could well lie in the wonders of humour – that rare ability to laugh at ourselves and with others. When we think of jokes, many of us think of, say, the Irish:

> Host: Hey Paddy, come over on Friday for a party. Don't worry about drinks, they're on the house.
> On Friday, Paddy turns up, carrying a ladder.
> Host: Hey Paddy, great you could make it. But what's with the ladder?

Paddy: Didn't you say drinks were on the house?

One has to be creative to both evoke laughter and enjoy a good laugh. I recall with a smile an advertisement I saw in Australia; it was an advertisement for XXXX Beer. It simply stated:

I read about the hazards of drinking, so I gave up reading.

I belong to that other group of people who are also the butt of many jokes: the Punjabis. And, without being immodest, I can say that the Punjabis are a hardworking and goal-oriented people who have done much to make what India is today. And yet, every Punjabi enjoys a good joke, especially if the joke is directed at ourselves! The language, Punjabi, is rife with witticisms and allows plenty of space for those who want to pun and use its rich resources to put people in their proper place through humour!

Whether it is work, study or even making love, I am sure the Irish and the Punjabis all enjoy a good comic strip, comedy show or cartoon. Why? Because, I think, behind these wonderful creations we sense someone like us who has that rare and special gift called creativity and is putting this to very good use (and maybe even laughing his or her way to many banks!).

Part of the problem, as I see it, is that many of us are afraid to be funny, act funny or talk funny because our respective cultures don't welcome it. I remember many years ago as I was about to be made a young don at the university, my head of department took me and my buddy Max le Blond aside and said, "It is well-known that you two enjoy jokes and laugh at every little thing you find funny … Listen, people around here won't like that very much, so watch where and when you laugh." Today Max and I often look back at such homilies and laugh. We ask ourselves, why, why did we all have to be so **tight**? That, by the way, is a word our young use to encapsulate the not-very-nice things about us adults. As the great Joshua Bell put it, "**You can get so tied up in what's right that you lose the music**." So let me end this by leaving you with a few more jokes to enjoy.

Here's the irreverent Woody Allen, one of the finest minds I know, saying his piece: "Having sex is like playing bridge. If you don't have a good partner, you'd better have a good hand."

Tom Clancy, the well-known writer, says in one of his many wisecracks: "I believe that sex is one of the most beautiful, natural, wholesome things that money can buy." (This one is not really all that funny, but it makes its point without rancour!)

As a young boy I was told that Henry Miller (author of supposedly "unholy" books such as *Tropic of Cancer* and *Tropic of Capricorn*, but for me also the one who authored one of the nicest books I've ever read, a sad, profoundly moving tale, *The Smile at the Foot of the Ladder*, and a very good, long-forgotten book on D. H. Lawrence) was not an author whom I should read too much. As I grew older I realized why. Here is a quote from this extraordinary and courageous writer: "The Bible contains 6 admonishments to homosexuals and 62 to heterosexuals. That doesn't mean that God doesn't love heterosexuals. It's just that they need more supervision."

Finally, here's one that simply defies all our expectations and familiarities: "Never be afraid to tell the world who you are" by *Anonymous*.

Introduction 3

I asked Catherine Lim, who is probably Singapore's best-known fiction writer, three questions pertaining to the writing of this book. The following are my questions and her responses.

1. Q: How would you define **creativity**? In your opinion is there a difference between being **creative** and being **innovative**?

   CL: Creativity is the ability to break free of all established norms and practice, even the tried and true. Innovation is just building on what is already there.

2. Q: What *single* factor spurred your creativity? Why? How?

   CL: Passion – almost an obsession to do what one must. I don't know if there is any "why" to creativity – passion is its own justification. As to the "how", again it seems too complex to describe – you simply allow the process to define itself as it goes along.

3. Q: Name an individual (relative, friend, historical figure) who has made a big impact on your creative life. How has he or she done so?

   CL: There really has not been *one* individual. I have been deeply influenced by people who were true to themselves and pursued their passion as something larger than themselves.

My good friend Michael Millard, author of such engaging books as *Leaving Japan* and *Jihad in Paradise*, tells me that:

Creative people are those whose ideas consistently and comfortably leave behind the constraining channels of their training, then move easily beyond synthesis into unknown territory. Such people delight in such exploration, and can reconstitute what they have found for others.

From time immemorial people have tried to define and understand creativity. They have rarely succeeded or come to any agreement. In different parts of the world and at different times, creativity has been defined differently, probably as suited by the powers that be or in accordance with the general feel of acceptance or at least with the ethos of the contexts in which the definitions found themselves.

It is best to attempt an understanding of creativity through specific illustrations. Let me begin by referring to the well-known and often-told story about two mothers claiming the same boy as their son. Whether the judge was King Solomon, a Chinese Emperor or an Indian Rajah does not detract from the kernel of the tale itself.

> *King/Emperor/Rajah*: So you both say this boy is your son?
> *Mothers*: Yes.
> *King/Emperor/Rajah*: Well, since there is no way of settling this dispute, the only way is to cut the boy exactly in half and let each of you have one half.
> One of the mothers (screaming): Nooooooo! Let her have the boy. It's okay!

Well most of us know the story – it has been told again and again to illustrate how the great king/emperor/rajah arrived at a solution to a most awkward problem (those were the days when there were no sophisticated paternity-testing technologies).

When we read Shakespeare's *The Merchant of Venice*, we come across the great scene where Portia, acting as Antonio's lawyer, is pleading for leniency from the Jew, Shylock, who has lent Antonio a lot of money and wants it back because the repayment date was due. Portia pleads for mercy; Shylock is adamant. Finally Portia says, "Okay, since you insist that the money be paid back as it is writ (agreed upon in writing), let's proceed." She calls the court official to come and start cutting that pound of flesh which the contract said was to be payment if Antonia defaulted. Just as the pound of flesh was about to be cut, Portia says, "Remember Shylock, the contract says a pound of flesh, so you shall have your pound of flesh but make sure there's not a drop of blood, not a single drop of blood." Boy! This is legal supremacy all right! Poor Shylock – how can he have his rightful pound of flesh without shedding a single drop of blood?

These two stories reveal what to me is **negative creativity** – the sense of a creative solution to a problem which has to be solved, a situation which demands resolution. We all possess this; if we think back we will find several instances during our own life when we have been creative (ingenious might be a better term) because we needed to get out of a difficult situation or ease ourselves out of a non-tenable position. As they say, necessity is the mother of all invention.

But this book is not concerned about negative creativity; if we all just wait for terrible life-and-death situations to occur before we start being creative, we would never have arrived at the state we are today because most of our achievements have been the result of individuals and groups of individuals taking it upon themselves to see and do things differently not because they were forced to, but because they sensed different ways of doing and saying things. Here we are concerned about **positive** creativity or creativity as a human driving force which impels us to create ideas, services and products which we feel will add to the rich storehouse of human fulfilment and glory.

Historically, creative people were frequently punished because their responses, positions or creations were seen to be going against the grain, running against official sanctions, expressing disbelief in the *status quo* or at least questioning authority. Of course I am simplifying the actual process for reasons of clarity and focus, but the point I am making is simple: creative people often did not receive due recognition or reward because those in a position to do this for them felt afraid, intimidated, threatened. Whether these were politicians, professors, managers, parents or religious pundits, whatever their profession, rank and role, these were people who felt that if they rewarded creative individuals, they might set the wheels of change in motion. Most cultures were afraid of change. Most cultures *are* afraid of change. Indeed, most of *us* are afraid of change. This is one explanation as to why we don't always agree on what is creative. When Wordsworth and Coleridge first published their famous *Lyrical Ballads*, Lord Jeffrey, their critic, immediately said, **"This will never do**." Note *"never"*. The likes of Lord Jeffrey were afraid that given the basic revolution in poetic diction, which this book was proposing, the entire well-being of English poetry would have been compromised, scandalized even! Hence every effort was made to dismiss the claims by these two poets. It literally took more than 200 years for most people to accept that poetry – and very good poetry at that – can be written in a language which is not necessarily immediately recognizable as **poetic**. On hindsight, the words of The Ancient Mariner say much:

> We were the first
> That ever burst
> Into that silent sea.

First bursts are often met with a great deal of suspicion. But there is some consolation in this context: Lord Jeffrey seems all but forgotten while the *Lyrical Ballads* live on!

Edward de Bono, the great lateral thinker who is world-famous for the many contributions he has made to this whole arena of creative thinking, stated in a message dated 4 June 2001 that the reason why for centuries no one had come up with the very simple idea of **thinking hats** (his idea) was:

> ... the guardians of intellectual process in society are so enamoured of the critical mode that there has been no effort to develop constructive modes of thinking.

And de Bono is right! For too long people have paid more attention to the **critical** mode than the creative. Why? Because the creative mode is an **upsetting** mode, it disturbs, it challenges, it introduces notions which threaten weak individuals (especially those in power and positions of authority) and, generally, the creative mode is too often associated with the idle, the restless, the anarchic, the **marginals** – people or groups of people who do not occupy **central** spaces in the society or community in which they find themselves. Also the critical mode is easier to handle; it is, supposedly, more **rational** than the creative! And we know that our educational system has usually stressed the left-brain modalities, and creativity belongs to the right brain. While it is easier to test the critical mode (say by using the famous imperatives of **logic**) it is much harder to test the creative mode (people always ask **who says this is creative?**) – in the latter there is not, as yet, a consensus.

I recall that when I was a first-year student at the then University of Singapore, Mr Lee Kuan Yew, the Prime Minister of the nation, told all of us freshmen that Singapore, because of its urgent priorities, could not afford the luxury of creative artists. We cannot afford to have poets sit under coconut trees and dream, said

Mr Lee. We need scientists, engineers, people who can build houses, hospitals, roads. And so for many years the creative side of things went unemphasized. Until one day we woke up to read in the newspapers a question asked by the then Foreign Minister (also the accepted **ideologue** of the ruling party): Where, asked Mr S. Rajaratnam (himself a writer) are Singapore's **dreamers**? Indeed! The point being that without dreamers and dreams, a nation very quickly loses its impetus, its steam. For any nation to grow, it must, *must* have its fair share of people who dream. Because, as they say, today's dreams are tomorrow's realities. The same Mr Lee who in 1969 had been quite blunt about the country's urgent needs, said recently that what had worked for his team for over 30 years was not going to work for the next 30 years; that Singapore needed a change of mindset, otherwise its very survival might be at stake. A new era. A new mindset. A change of paradigm.

De Bono, in a webpage message dated 24 March 2003, said that our idea of a thinking culture has been primarily based on **judgement**; that is, we tend to judge more than we allow for the creative free flow of ideas. How often have we ourselves been prone to this sort of judgement-paradigm? How often have we, when someone close to us approach us with a new idea, uttered, "**That's crazy – that won't work!**" Or, how often have we chided those near and dear to us for wasting time by doing nothing, just idling. I know so many parents who just cannot watch their children do nothing; they want their kids to be always doing something, doing something, that is, in their judgement, worth doing. Because we all know that no one really does nothing. When people see us as doing nothing we are frequently really daydreaming, or just enjoying the breeze or the clouds, or whatever, a reverie! But those around us don't like that; it worries them, it threatens their hold on reality.

Now, Edward de Bono's remarkable theories of creativity and his many insights into the nature of creative thought helped bring about a greater awareness of the need and the possibility of **training** people to be creative. Using his famous **6 Thinking Hats**, for example, de Bono illustrated how we can gear our minds towards a more creative way of sensing the world and acting in it. Though it cannot be said that de Bono is the first person to discuss creativity in a manner which makes a lot of sense and contributes to a reassessment of the modalities by which we make sense of reality, it can be said that almost single-handedly, de Bono did much to revolutionize the entire arena of creative thinking. I have learnt a lot from this genius and I am prepared to say that without de Bono, we would have been terribly impoverished. But we now need to go beyond de Bono because, in the main, I don't think de Bono has addressed the issue of creativity across cultures, creatively or emphatically. And I think we must.

My colleague Dawn Dekle who teaches Psychology at the Singapore Management University says, "**Kirpal, think: de Bono's hats belong to a "mono-culture", your coloured turbans belong to a "multi-culture."** Creativity and creative thinking demands self-fulfilment; creative individuals tend to be stubborn precisely because they feel their ideas are very important. Of course they may be wrong – they often are. But what is significant here is not that creative persons are many a time proven wrong but that they even have the courage (the gall, the gumption, the arrogance) to articulate their beliefs or ideas in the first place. Too many systems obstruct and place restraints on creative individuals; in almost every society these restrictions are present. After all we have all heard of the teacher who said to the six-year-old girl who had painted an object **black** and called it an apple, "There are no black apples, my dear child – draw that apple again."

And so we keep drawing that green apple to make our teachers, our parents, our spouses, our bosses, our friends happy. And in doing this we lose precisely that which makes us different and gives us that creative edge. What is needed now is to bring back that old confidence which gave birth to great thinkers like Christ, Buddha, Mohammad, Nanak, Confucius. We talk about men and women who sacrifice their all in order to make our lives better; men and women who light up our lives through their music, songs, dance, poems, stories, inventions, discoveries. Well, we can be like them. We can bond. We can triumph. But we must first acknowledge that to be creative involves staking a claim, claiming ownership, and putting our money where our creativity is. Are we all sure we want to do this? History has shown that creative individuals are usually recognized long after their essential creativity has been expressed and because of this, few truly live happily or become rich and famous. For every Newton, Einstein or Bill Gates there are thousands who never make it, at least not during their lifetime.

One of Singapore's more successful entrepreneurs is Inderjit Singh, Member of Parliament and author of a forthcoming book on entrepreneurship. When I asked him what his take on creativity was, he responded as follows:

> Creativity has got a lot to do with a curious mind and a mind which thinks out of the box. Curiosity leads people to experiment with different ideas and alternatives. They think about things which people will not normally think about. They are willing to question the *status quo*. They ask the question differently from others. Instead of asking 'Why?', they typically ask 'Why Not?'. By not placing a limit to what they can do or think of and by not practising 'self-censorship' of their minds, they are able to come out with ideas which very few can dream of. Talking about dreams, yes, creative people have to be dreamers and they dream of not just 'airy fairy' things, but also about ideas which can revolutionize the industry or even the world.

Well, there you go. Take it from those who have made good through persistence. Inderjit speaks of dreams which will revolutionize the world, that is, make a tremendous impact on people. Yes. This is what the best of creative minds have achieved.

Allow me to end this chapter with a narrative, a story. Think about it as you continue this journey.

> There was once a man who wanted everyone to know just how clever he was. So he invented a new way of drinking water. People were intrigued. Wow, they said, this man must be truly clever, no one in 200 years has come up with a new way of drinking water. So the man's reputation grew and more and more people from around the globe started to clamour for him. The man himself grew more and more sure of himself. He became rich and famous. He was highly sought after. Everything seemed to go his way. Then one day the man's luck ran out. Suddenly there was no more water. And because there was no more water, no one wanted this man anymore. Indeed they began to think that the cause for the lack of water was this man's new way of drinking it. They began to affirm their conviction that they were right. The poor man was cursed. His name appeared in all the world's media.

The people wanted him tried for deceit, theft and corrupt practices. Seeing all of this, the man went to the top of a mountain and said, "**Here I am – let the gods use my body and turn my bones and flesh into water for the people down there.**" And so it was that the rains started again. And people had water. And they drank it the way they had always drunk it. The man whom they now drank no longer existed.

Introduction 4

For everything that lives is holy.

Thank God I was never sent to school
To be flogged into becoming a fool.

I must create my own system or be enslaved by that of another man's.

All three of these statements come from the pen of one of the world's greatest artists: William Blake. Anyone who knows even a little about this strange and mysterious man will know just how creative he was and just how different he was, and how much he suffered on account of this. For Blake, everything was at stake: religion, nation, earth, poetry, art, love, friendship, people. Blake believed in the power of the Imagination. More than even the later Romantics, it was Blake, I think, who gave the English poetic landscape the freedom and the push it needed to move forward. More than the fearful symmetry, Blake gave a new dimension to the language. When it didn't serve his purpose, he, like Shakespeare before him, invented new words and new phrases or used old and familiar words and phrases with totally new and distinct meanings. Because Blake was more radical, he was more daring than the Bard. And he was certainly not as diplomatic. Readers then and now have complained about Blake's mystical visions, his peculiar symbols (even a seemingly common symbol like the **rose** becomes in Blake's hands a symbol of something universally forceful and terrifying), his daring insights, his frightening drawings and designs, his strange utterances (many of my students used to be puzzled as to why I always began my lectures on Blake by citing such statements as, "Every harlot was a virgin once" when I wanted, deliberately, to make them sit up and reflect on the hypocrisy which surrounded them as it did in Blake's own time), his private ruminations. This man could serve, as many others I suppose have served and will serve, as the **prime** example and instance of **creative**

genius. In many ways this small book is a tribute to one such as Blake. For I have travelled many journeys with Blake and, like him, I have tried to reach that state of higher Innocence where the marriage of heaven and hell is complete. The testimonies of those who have tried to fathom what Blake was truly about – the great Blake scholars like Northrop Frye and Harold Bloom – have said it more than once: here is a writer, a visionary from whose life and work every one of us can glean gems of wisdom. In the great code of our mundane, routine everyday living we no longer have time for the likes of Blake; he is too difficult, too alien to our contemporary sensibility. And yet, I would attest, he helped shape and formulate the bedrocks of our modern sense of freedom and free space. I know that my own life changed after I confronted his work and engaged with what others had written about him. Today, in many of the more enlightened circles of management theory, the works of Blake may yet return to help and assist in the clear thinking of a new philosophy of global business conduct. I affirm the relevance, now more than ever, of a revisitation of this great man's poetry, his illuminating artwork and his liberating philosophy. I affirm we need Blake to show us the way. I affirm Blake illustrates what creativity is – in his life, his writings, and his achievements. The world has yet to fully acknowledge William Blake's full contribution to our changed concepts of freedom and knowledge. The world has yet to acknowledge what creativity is truly about.

THE CULTURAL FACTOR

Is it true that certain societies tend to be more **creative** than others? That certain communities display a greater desire, drive or willingness to try out new ideas, new adventures, new things? That certain groups of human beings, singly or collectively, tend to be more creative-driven?

History tells us that the old civilizations demonstrated an impressive capacity to be innovative, creative, adventurous, daring and risk-taking. The Old World of Egypt, Greece, Rome, Arabia, Persia, China, India, Peru, and older still, Mesopotamia and Sumeria, all showed true grit when it came to doing new things, and doing things differently. The Hanging Gardens of Babylon, the Great Wall of China, the Pyramids, the Colossus in Rome and the myriads of achievements of the Old World, which most of us know only through reading history, all testify to the creative spirit inherent in these ancient civilizations.

Yes, I believe certain societies do have a greater creative drive than others. Admittedly, it was easier, on the whole, to be more creative in times past; life was neater and simpler, with ample scope for new creations. The march of time has meant that more and more peoples have been pushed and forced to think of newer and newer ways to survive and progress, so much so that nowadays it is very hard to claim uniqueness and singular distinction. Indeed, as I constantly tell my students every time they seek my approval for new, creative projects as part of their group assignments, with each passing semester **originality** and **difference** become more and more strenuous, more difficult to realize. Hence the common error of thinking that adaptation equals creativity, that things modified are things newly born.

For decades Japan was, undoubtedly, the premier nation in terms of adapting and modifying services and products to impress the world and international markets. The Japanese took, say, a radio and voilà, a hundred new radios were created, smaller, sleeker, better – and they did this with almost every new technology and technological product. The rest of the world bought Japanese cars, television sets and washing machines – and Japan grew richer and richer. Even in the very sophisticated industries of computer manufacturing the Japanese excelled in their distinctively designed products.

Then came the crash. Japan lost its edge, its cutting edge. Just like the civilizations of yore, Japan had to come to terms with the fact that its **creative** or **innovative** energy was somehow missing. It became aware, very aware, of the fact that adaptation and modification in themselves do not and cannot be substitutes for genuine creativity and innovation. The Japanese are now trying to get back on their feet. But as the old pop song goes, "It's gonna take some time this time..."

What drives the creative society? What distinguishes it from a society that chiefly adapts and modifies? How do we recognize a creative people? What are the hallmarks of a community which is primarily creative?

These are tough questions. They are sensitive questions which, if answered wrongly, may lead to enormous misunderstanding. But certain truths need to be confronted and engaged with. For me, the answers to all of these questions lie, fundamentally, in what I call the **cultural factor**, those elements which contribute to the making of the overall **psyche**.

Countless debates and discussions have not settled the issue of what **culture** is. I will not enter into this here except to state that for me, five basic categories of culture contribute to the level of creativity in any civilization, society, community, group and nation. If we simply take culture to mean all that results in a certain trait among groups of people, that which underlines the conduct and behaviour of groups of people, then the following five aspects of culture surely play a vital role and will have to be reckoned with. As we go along let us bear in mind that very few societies, nations, communities or groups of people truly engage with their cultural contexts in a frank, truthful and robust manner, mainly because honest confrontation and engagement with them tend to result in anxieties, fears and apprehensions. So as we move along, let us be mindful. But let us also consider and reflect upon the implications so that we, as individuals, can have a better understanding of, and perhaps even a better grip on, the situation.

1. Family – The Biological Culture

It would appear that apart from a few very blessed persons – and even this is arguable – most of us have no choice insofar as everything connected with our birth is concerned. We do not choose the time or place that we were born, or our parents. So we come into the world and, as many philosophers have commented, **we cry that we have come to this great stage of fools**. In a well-known Hindi film, *Mera Naam Joker* (*My Name is Joker*), the following question is posed and acted out for over three hours: why does a baby's cry make everyone around happy at the time of birth? I leave the reader to ponder and puzzle over this because, truly, there is no single answer save for the baby's cry signals life!

We are born with a definite biology. We have no say over our genetic make-up – well, not unless it has been interfered with through cloning, hormone injection or chemical intake – and thus our **biological culture** is pre-determined. Some individuals and communities seem to have genes which are tougher, more resilient and perhaps even more inclined towards creativity; i.e., the chromosomes which assist the growth of the right side of the brain are more dominant than those which assist the left side. Now I am not a neuro-anybody so I do not lay claim to knowing what really goes on. But my suspicion is that some families just have better genes than others; some societies as a whole have better genes than others. And this gets the creative thingy going. Some years ago when the huge eugenics debate was on-going the controversy was very marked; this is a highly sensitive topic and rarely does anyone come out and say what he or she truly feels. But I believe that the family or biological culture has plenty to do with our personality and certainly explains why some tend to be more highly charged about creativity than others.

2. Learning – The Educational Culture

As we grow up we are sent to nurseries, kindergartens, schools, colleges and universities. All of these institutions play a pre-eminent role in the shaping of our sensibilities. For too long, in most societies, educational training has basically focused on the three Rs – reading, writing and arithmetic. In one way or another, all our early learning can be grouped under these three crucial tools of

knowledge, as it were. From the start the growing child learns to do things in a given manner. All over the world, children are **taught** how to sit, stand, write, read, talk, eat, drink, etc. No wonder then that every time children get the chance, they deviate, moving away from what the elders are teaching them (and what they are supposed to be learning and picking up!) and doing things their own way! The English poet, William Blake, one of my heroes, put it quite bluntly:

> Thank God I was never sent to school
> To be flogged into becoming a fool!

Maybe the fact that Blake, who was largely self-taught, wrote some wonderfully memorable lyrics (for example, *How I roamed from field to field*) by the time he was just aged 14, ought to suggest something deep and meaningful to us. The way we teach our young, the **educational culture**, in other words, is of the utmost significance in terms of why some societies tend to become more creativity-driven. The world-famous Montessori system, which allows for enormous freedom, is now coming in vogue again because more and more parents are realizing that the major educational institutions of today somehow tend not to stress the innovative and creative aspects of experience and learning.

Studies have shown that children tend to be very creative; about 98% of them display creative characteristics. Hence if we just leave kids alone, within minutes they are able to devise games and preoccupying activities. As children grow up and get more and more educated, ironically their creative side tends to diminish. So that, as studies show, by the time they graduate, only about 20% seem to be creative. Alas, by age 40–45 years (i.e., the age when we feel we have reached a stage when we can make decisions!) only about 3% retain that creative drive. I have witnessed parent after parent trying hard to place their children in schools which show high examination success rates. Indeed, I can share my personal experience of this. My three daughters were all enrolled in Singapore's noted Catholic school – Marymount. We enrolled our girls there because Marymount Kindergarten and Marymount Convent were known for two main things: (a) free-play, and (b) proficiency in English. Thus Marymount girls almost always had a flair for conversation and were known for their social ease, as well as a certain "naughtiness", which meant that they were cheeky and often behaved in slightly out-of-the-normal ways. Within a very few years we were troubled as more and more parents demanded that the teachers gave more homework to the kids (mind you, I am talking about kids in kindergarten and Primary 1 and 2). Under tremendous parental pressure, the principal finally gave in. And the one school we thought was different as far as just getting good examination grades was concerned, finally caved in before the parents would take their children out and leave the school bereft of pupils! Alas, this was a very sad time. We then decided to have our girls educated in Australia, where I am proud to say, they continue to receive an excellent all-round education even if their specific subject grades are not anywhere near those of their Singaporean counterparts.

Here is an interesting question: do students who achieve superlative examination grades (the As and the even better A+s) manifest a greater tendency to be creative? I have my doubts. If truth were known, I think I will be vindicated in my belief that good examination grades frequently work against the creative grain because good examination marks are usually dependent upon a preordained order of response(s). Again this is debatable and I am offering a hunch. Perhaps more research could be done in this direction? From my experience of facilitating the Creative Thinking module at the Singapore Management University, I know that the students who usually obtain B+ and C+ grades tend to be more active in coming up with original creative ideas. On a lighter note I once asked a former education minister in Singapore that given the extremely high number of As we have scored in examinations such as the Cambridge O-levels and A-levels, surely Singapore should have bagged a few world awards such as the Nobel and the Pulitzer. The minister looked at me quizzically before laughing and saying, "**I get your meaning but mass education cannot cater just to the select few.**" It is useful to note, in passing, that revered educational institutions such as Cambridge University and Harvard University are fast changing their outlook in order to keep up with the demands of this new age. Both have appointed women to significant positions for the first time in their respective 600- and 300-year history.

The educational culture is crucial to the level of creativity found in a society, community or group. At one level this is so commonsensical that writing about it becomes silly, and yet I know that this is a major factor in all discussions and even theories about creativity. How we educate our children and how our young learn are instrumental in their later ability to think and act creatively. From basic activities such as colouring an apple either green or red to more elaborate activities such as drawing a doctor in a coat (as opposed to say, jeans) or a priest in robes (as opposed to say, jeans!), our educational culture imposes a given way of doing things rightly or wrongly, and therefore blocks alternatives. If a child draws a black apple or a black pear or a black orange, he or she gets chided for not knowing the right colours of the fruit. It is as simple and basic as this. The sooner we allow for more freedom in our children's learning, the quicker we will see creative results!

3. Playing – The Sociological Culture

Outside the family, school and college, who do we play with, socialize with, eat and drink with, jog with, watch movies with or travel with? If we were to seriously examine the kinds of people we mingle and mix with outside our formalized time, we can, I believe, get a clear index of the push or drive for creativity and innovation. Thus if we were to mix with individuals from a strong creative-driven biological culture coupled with individuals from a positive creativity-inspiring or nurturing educational culture, then we will, ourselves, be spurred to become creative. It is true that human beings love to do what we see each other doing. We are, yes, a herd – we simply love to conform, to get safety in numbers. Alas, given our family and learning contexts we usually mix with others of our kind, those of the same ilk. The result? More of the same!

One of the many experiments I used to try with my daughters as they were growing up was almost always to take them to markedly different places where the kinds of environment they encountered were often beyond their ken. Thus I took them to the wild landscapes of Pahang and Kelantan where, in the night, we went out with matches and candles, listening to the cicadas as well as looking out for wild deer. I took them to the side streets of poverty-stricken *kampungs* in Malaysia, Indonesia and the Philippines, to show them how young people elsewhere managed their lives and their learning. The main thrust behind all of these odd outings was simple: in getting to know other kinds of living conditions and lifestyles we would better appreciate ours as well as learn from others how, creatively, we could achieve much with very little. Because the belief in so many advanced and developed societies is that the more money we have, the better our ability for innovation and creativity. On the contrary, it is usually the less privileged ones, the poorer ones who display more agility in being able to survive and even beat the system. They do this in ingeniously creative ways, often landing themselves in dire straits because they flout rules and regulations in the process. However, as is now becoming quite apparent, societies which limit behaviour by saying, "**This is what you can do**," (i.e., one cannot, say, do a U-turn unless told to do so by a legal sign!) tend to be less creative than those who just say, "**This is what you cannot do**," (i.e., you can do a U-turn anywhere except where there is a legal sign saying NO U-TURN). The point is most of us in the so-called developed or first world do not often think it is wise to expose our young to those from other worlds! Hence our young grow up playing and mingling with others whose life patterns are recognizably similar to ours. Again conformity or sameness takes away the drive to be different and creative. In a bold move to nurture and encourage difference Singapore is now proposing a varied **sociological culture** in which differences are celebrated, rather than merely tolerated, or worse, lamented! Many of the old taboos are being removed, and new exciting activities and ventures are being introduced. The idea is that when the sociological culture is exciting, the creative spirit will be enhanced.

4. Working – The Career Culture

Someone said that for most human beings these days only two activities dominate: working and sleeping! All other things we do fall into the broad time frames allowed for by and between our sleeping and our working. Where do we work? Who do we work with? What kind of systems are in place where we work? What kind of bosses do we work for? These and related questions contribute to what I term the **career culture**. Because we spend so much time at our workplace or simply working, it becomes imperative that the main driving forces of the environment we are in will have an impact on our creative drive or ability. Most work organizations like government agencies and ministries seek obedience from their employees. Desperately few employers allow or encourage diversity. Conformity is the order of the day, and precious few would want to challenge this because we have mouths to feed and bodies to clothe!

The work ethic of such famous organizations as 3M, Microsoft, Hewlett-Packard, Toyota and MIT, and the **new** players in the field from the point of view of creativity such as Citibank and Creative Technology, is legendary for the freedom of time and space they allow their employees (in some cases, **some** rather than all of the employees) to think of new, creative ideas which will help keep the organizations always ahead of their competitors. I am told that in places such as 3M, workers get, sometimes, up to 30% time-off in order to facilitate free time for thinking, sharing and simply, brainstorming. Too many of our employers are under the constraints of delivery i.e., **getting things done** so much so that the need for allowing free time and space for people to come up with new ways and means of doing things or new and exciting products is not catered for. Though many organizations pay thousands and thousands of dollars to invite experts to conduct creativity training for their staff, they do not follow up on this or put what they have learnt into practice because they cannot allow themselves to believe that giving employees time-off will result in someone somewhere coming up with fantastic ideas for the organizations to stay ahead. We are, most of us, enslaved by the work habits of the past and refuse to chart new territories. Encumbered by daily routine and rituals, we prevent ourselves from taking it easy and therefore from allowing ourselves simply to relax and have the sheer physical energy to think creatively. My constant experience with my undergraduate students is that every time I give them time-off to think, they invariably return with very creative ideas.

Our career culture, therefore, needs to be more positively aligned to the needs and demands of creativity and innovation. Every organization should try and suss out who among the employees is potentially keen and able to think of creative ideas. Such employees should be given plenty of room to manoeuvre. Time and time again we hear of success stories of people giving up on their workplaces and setting up shop on their own because their erstwhile bosses just didn't want to listen to their original ideas! There is a whole new world waiting out there, no matter what work we are doing. From the much-revered halls of religious practices to the exacting corridors of the legal and medical fraternities, everywhere there is a genuine cry for new and innovative ways of doing things. Our career culture must nourish us and give us the wherewithal to foray into new territory and creatively find solutions to our existing problems or discover new possibilities for us to work on.

5.   Loving – The Sexual Culture

Most of us feel loneliness when it hits us. By nature we are gregarious creatures. Each and every one of us yearns, often, for a partner, that super-special person who will help us fulfil all our dreams and make living exciting and good. In ancient societies partners were usually chosen or pre-determined by a variety of rituals – usually under the authority of the elders. These days most of us like to choose our partners on our own. With more and more legitimacy provided to accommodate all manner of coupling nowadays, lovers are well able to select and settle with individuals of their liking. Most of us have little or no time for the old ways of getting people together. Astrology and related arts no longer fuel our imagination. We prefer the rational approach, even if the origin of the approach is purely passion. Who do we marry? Why?

I have often thought about this. Here is an aspect of life which most of us would not want to connect with creativity or the spirit of innovation. And yet it seems only too clear to me that if our sexual culture is wrong, that is, if we end up with the wrong partners, our own creativity invariably suffers. I am under the impression that whether we like it or not, the old forms of getting couples married did serve a commendable end: individuals were chosen based upon what I have termed above, essentially, the biological and educational cultures. Thus it was extremely rare for a doctor to marry a servant, a soldier to marry a professor or a dancer to marry a lawyer. These days all of these partnerships are acceptable. I am not sure if, given such configurations, I'd go all the way for the old systems. No. But what I do know is that if the **cultures** of the coupling individuals are such that at every turn and corner there is a clash, then Huntington's predictions are sure to come true! The clash will be real and very, very painful. So much so that the tremendous energy which ought to go into creativity goes instead into fights and arguments. Yes, we read fantastic tales of people going the extra mile to think of very creative ways to punish their straying partners, but alas, these are exercises in negative creativity. And the end result is, usually, very, very sad.

I believe that if we choose and have the good blessings to be with a partner who understands truly what we are about, who knows and feels for us, who fundamentally shares our vision and values and above all who is ready and prepared to give us that extra space and room for us to think and act, then we are in the right sexual culture. And this will in itself allow us to think and behave more creatively. I have observed couples over a lifetime and can firmly say that couples who **menace** each other at every given opportunity (i.e., argue, fight and rationalize) tend to make each other small and diminish each other's confidence, and with this, the creative drive, the innovative spirit. As we read the accounts of the great creative geniuses, again and again it becomes evident that the support and love given by that one special person in our lives contribute one heck of a lot to our own capacity for a creative outlet. Couples who do not always work to a routine, couples who always allow space for spontaneity, couples who always accommodate a third or fourth person without fuss and irritation – these tend to produce more levels of creative energies. Again this is and will appear to many to be sheer common sense. But we know that for most of us common sense, or rather the lack of it, is the final and real enemy.

Most people, when they think of culture or cultural factors usually think of matters like ethnicity and religion. But it is also critical to note the several other cultures which influence and impact our attitudes, beliefs and values – such as the five outlined above. These days we hear people talking about their school culture, their family culture, their corporate culture. Many years ago I mooted the idea of establishing a Centre for Cross-Cultural Studies. This was eventually set up, after the usual merry-go-round. I was told that important decisions take a long time to be made and then acted upon! (Note: Creative ideas in this day and age cannot, repeat, cannot wait too long – the ideas get hijacked!) We had recently, the case of Mr Sim Wong Hoo, boss of Creative Technologies, saying the reason why he chose to tie up with a Malaysian university rather than a Singaporean one was that he did not have to wait very long to get things going! When I formulated the frame of reference for the centre I used the world **culture** in a broad, loose sense so that we could talk about the culture of the young versus the culture of the old, the culture of beauty versus the culture of ugliness, and so on. But almost *all* my colleagues told me to stick to the normal or traditional understanding of culture, which was a pity because I thought (and still do think) that this would inevitably reduce the scope of the centre's activities and importance. But the fact that today people are already starting to talk about different kinds or modes of culture is a healthy sign. It means that in addition to the usual cultural dimensions people are taking into consideration, many other factors that play a vital and significant role. It is never too late to learn. And for some of us, for reasons best known to ourselves, learning is important and accelerated because of the **who** factor; i.e., if someone we respect or someone in authority (yes, especially here in Singapore!) tells us to do so, we are very quick to respond and react. Alas, many of those in authority take too long to make up their minds or give the benefit of the doubt to us poor sods, who may have the ideas but not the pull or influence and certainly not the authority. Indeed, it has been my own experience that people with creative ideas are sometimes not even given positions of authority because of the fear that "**they may not follow our bidding or instructions**". And it is *this* slavish culture which always pays heed to rules and regulations that kill and destroy the spirit of creativity. Hard to swallow, even harder to publicly embrace, but this is the sad truth.

But, hey, maybe all is not lost – as my friends in the various drinks industry might add, "What about our yogurt culture?"

The LANGUAGE QUESTION

As far as I know no one in the world has, as yet, discussed the issue of language with regard to creativity. I mean no one has tried to discover or explore the link between language – its structure, lexicon, rules and grammar – and its impact on an individual's creative thinking and action. This is a difficult relationship to even verbalize so this first excursion into serious, tough, almost taboo areas might prove unduly provocative. But I am going to stick my turban out and say coloured turbans one day led me to think and reflect on the ways in which the language(s) we are brought up in influence our creativity. I believe some languages are more **creativity-enlivening**; others are more **creativity-deadening**.

First some examples are in order. Many years ago, around 1966, I wrote the following in a school magazine:

Lounge Hostess approaches gentleman sitting in a lounge chair.
Lounge Hostess: Sir, are you relaxing?
Gentleman: No, Miss, I am Kirpal Singh.

Corny. Very, very corny. And yet, it inevitably makes people laugh. English has this capacity – words can be used in such a way that they can bring a smile upon a face even when the utterance is corny. Here are two more examples of linguistic humour, albeit what my daughters will term, "**Weak, Daddy, weak**.":

Teacher: Jane, why are you doing your math sums on the floor?
Jane: Oh, because you told me not to use tables!

Teacher: If I have seven apples in my left hand and eight apples
in my right hand, what do I have?
Jeremy: Two very big hands!

Now, let me ask you, my dear reader, first what language you are most comfortable with and whether this language impels you to be creative, i.e., it invites you to make up jokes. I am not a linguist but here are some of my speculations which I would truly like language scientists to explore because I firmly believe the link between language and creativity could provide us with a crucial key to opening up the myriad mysteries of creativity.

Thus, I think Spanish is more creative than, say, English. Think of all the great Spanish writers (let's just start with Cervantes – my friends tell me that no English translation of *Don Quixote* comes even remotely close to the richness of the puns and metaphors used in the original) and reflect upon the fact these writers (think of more modern examples like Borges and Marquez) don't just write wonderfully powerful fiction and poems, they also **create** new literary forms or sub-forms and genres. I am not going to go into Spanish music or Spanish inventions here but I do want to invite my readers to do so: take some time to think about the many different ways in which, because the Spanish language is so richly **pro**-creativity, speakers of it seem to have enormous creative push, drive and energy.

What about Italian? My primitive view is that it is perhaps not as liberally creativity-enlivening as Spanish (because of its Catholic bedrock springing from its links to Latin, a dead language which probably died because it didn't have the creative edge to survive the onslaught of time and a different religious ethos) but certainly more than English. After all, Italians burst into song every moment they can; they seem to be born poets and Bocaccio's tales seem so much more fun than Chaucer's inventive imitations. (Before I get killed by those who claim expertise in these sensitive areas let me say that all of what I am saying here is like virgin territory – there is pain to be experienced on all sides and fronts!) When I was in Rome in 2001 I took the liberty of asking a man on the street near the ancient ruins of the Colossus whether he thought Italian as a language was creative. "Of course, of course," he answered with hundreds of gesticulations, "yes, more, much more than all other languages, better than French, German, English, maybe even better than – where you come from?" I laughed, telling him I came from India (in Rome a little fibbing can often go a long way!) and he said, "Yes, Indian." Well, I was not about to correct him about that **Indian** *faux pas* but thanked him and walked on (though, to finish this anecdote, it took me some 45 minutes eventually to say good-bye to my Italian friend, so friendly was his demeanour!)

I don't know much about French and German. For me both of these languages do not appear to be as creativity-enlivening as English. My belief is simply based on the understanding that both of these languages have such fixed rules, such fixed grammatical applications, so much so that divergence literally is punished by non-acknowledgement, that chances of them encouraging a pro-creative stance are rare. I may be mistaken and therefore stand corrected and plead indulgence from those who know better. But I do most earnestly want the experts to start **testing** my simple hypothesis – that languages which have a very heavy structure base cannot prove to be very creativity-enlivening. In respect of French there was an interesting report some years ago about how the conservatives, the custodians of the French language and culture were most distressed about the intrusion of **English** words and phrases into French discourse. They blamed it on, among other things, McDonald's! Well, maybe this, too, supports my contention – after all McDonalds has been extremely successful, nudging out, perhaps, some more staid French fast-food chains!

Nearer home, which is Singapore, though I am not too fluent in all of our four official languages (English, Malay, Tamil and Mandarin), I venture to make some wild, speculative guesses. One of my many blessings has been that in the first ten years of my schooling I studied all the four official languages though I cannot say that I know them all equally well. I have tested my theories with several people, ranging from colleagues at the university to learned professors from other universities to people whom I meet at dinners or lunches. I think the most pro-creative language among the four has to be Malay. Anyone listening to Malay being spoken will immediately note that it is musical (akin to Spanish and Italian) and seems to have very fluid contextual rules. Thus a simple word like *sayang* can have so many meanings and nuances that most of us give up, as it were, trying to pin the word down to anything. I cannot find an equivalent in Mandarin or Tamil or even English. On descending order here is my theory: Malay, English, Mandarin, Tamil. Why is Tamil last? Because I think Tamil gets lost in its insistence on being correct rather than communicative. Tamil's closeness to Sanskrit – like Latin, another dead language today – might also help explain some of its deadening effects.

Pause.

So Susan reaches heaven's gate and there to greet her is St Peter.

"Good morning, Susan," he says.

"Good morning," returns Susan, "this is wonderful. All my life I have tried to be good so that one day I could be in heaven. And now I am here."

"Good," says St Peter, "but I'm afraid I can't let you in, Susan."

"Why?" asks Susan in total disbelief at the Gatekeeper's audacity.

"Well, simple. Look at the way you are dressed. You are half-naked," says St Peter, pointing to Susan's naked breasts.

"But I have a divine right," insists Susan.

St Peter calmly replies, "Both are divine, Susan, but I still can't let you in."

So, can a joke like this be told ravishingly in Mandarin? My friends tell me, not really – well, not in contemporary Mandarin. My view is that Mandarin is a fairly **closed** language, more eager to uphold its **purity** than its flexibility. Just like French or German. What makes languages like Malay and English very pro-creativity, it seems to me, is their ability to appropriate words from anywhere and everywhere and not flinch. These languages just pick up words not extant in their own lexicon and carry on using these newly acquired words and phrases as if they've always belonged. A learned Mandarin scholar tells me that unlike contemporary Mandarin, **old Mandarin, is different; it is very creative**. It could be. But I am here merely speaking about contemporary Mandarin as it is learnt, studied and taught in Singapore schools. Indeed, I suspect that if someone were to do a scientific study or survey they might well find that since tiny Singapore started its Speak Mandarin Campaign, the noticeable level of creative expression has declined, perhaps even proportional to the Singaporean's acquisition of Mandarin! Now there are, of course, lots of creative individuals in China but if one uses a gauge relative to the population, I think it'd be easy to see where I am coming from. I mean there are many more creative individuals in, say, the US or the UK than there are in China or even, for that matter, in India (where hundreds of languages compete for attention). Now, I also happen to believe that Chinese **dialects** are very creativity-enlivening. I fondly remember how as a young boy I used to listen to all the stories being broadcast on Rediffusion and how Chinese grannies and aunties would sit in rapt silence. When they later retold these stories to those who had missed the direct broadcasts, very interesting variations were infused. I can attest to this myself because in those days – and even now – I was quite at ease conversing in a dialect like Hokkien, one of the more widely used dialects in Singapore!

I believe one easy way of establishing just how creativity-enlivening a language is, is to look at its vocabulary and, perhaps with the help of a concordance, to check just how many words there are which relate to and help define, say, the notion of **individual** and **individuality**, and how distinct they are from **community** and **society**. In English there are more words for describing the individual and individuality than community and society. While not 100% definite, it does indicate that a language having more words for the individual would, prima facie, be more pro-creative. I think the same might apply to Spanish, Italian and Malay – the languages I consider to be more creativity-enlivening.

This has been one of the more **problematic** sections of this book because almost all of it is based on a hunch. As a final test to see if this hunch is indeed legitimate (and to help tease my readers, particularly those who might by now be so irked they want to get rid of me or at least burn this book), I invite my Mandarin-speaking friends to translate the following statement and see whether the same **tonalities** remain:

> The one good thing about the future is that it comes one day at a time.
>
> *Abraham Lincoln*

Do they? Does the Mandarin translation convey or capture both the funny as well as the sad side of this ruefully wise statement? (Note: When I asked a teacher-friend for a translation of Lincoln's statement she had to refer to two other Mandarin speakers before a translation was forthcoming. And even then, they said, "Translations cannot capture the original, not, especially, its wit.") My Mandarin-speaking friends confirm that it is easier to translate a sentence like, "**In politics there are no permanent friends, only permanent interests.**" Does this help to make my point? And, by the way, is it not true that the great creative poets of the Sung and

Tang Dynasties didn't pass their Imperial examinations – those questions on the Four Books of the great Confucius? Now, did they fail because they were stupid, unprepared or too creative in their responses?) Think also how English has been used to engage, for hundreds of years, our attention: for example, Shakespeare's "Friends, Romans, Countrymen, lend me your ears," Martin Luther King's "I have a dream", Tennyson's "...tears, tears, tears what do they mean?"

> So the former President of the Philippines, Estrada (popularly known as Erap) is asked by a visiting journalist: "Mr President, now that some time has passed since all the problems associated with your Presidency, what, can you say, finally brought you down?" The ex-President thinks for a while and finally replies: "You know, to be totally frank, I think it was the **coup de text**."

Brilliant! See how the English language is so flexible and while colonizing words from other languages (which it has famously done for centuries!) it creates a unique new idiom, phrase or word! Creative. Very creative. This may just be the place to say a few words about the issue of creativity versus cleverness. Creativity, as is commonly understood, refers to things or ideas which are original. Cleverness, on the other hand, usually refers to variations upon creative ideas/words/thoughts. Thus, in the very competitive world of modern advertising, those so-called creative directors often play upon images and words to come up with enticingly clever statements and taglines. I saw, in Sydney, the Virgin Blue airline (now Richard Branson IS a very creative and innovative guy!) advertise itself by catering to **movers and savers** (remember the original – movers and shakers?). Here are a few more examples of these clever variations I've collected:

> My next book is going to be called Harry Porter and the Philosopher's Scone.

> In discussing certain very feminine aspects of sexuality we have to reflect on a Tale of Two Titties.

> Because our poor Alice became distracted in Wonderland, we will have to rewrite her story under the title Alice in Pizzaland.

Clever people like to show off and clever modifications of words and phrases very often become a good way to impress others. I, myself, have built up a small collection of what I call *Kirpal's Aphorisms*. An example is "Blessed are the meek for they shall inherit the earth and nothing but the earth." Another one: Since it is always more blessed to give than receive, let me give you my troubles, worries and debts. In all of these we recognize the original which was the true creative expression; the clever ones acknowledge their due by their inability to make us forget where the originals come from. Since creativity is going to be increasingly rewarded, it is imperative that we learn to discriminate between creativity and cleverness and give real credit where this is merited.

Over to you, my dear reader, and if I err, please blame the very naughty Alice, who both in her Wonderland as well as her Looking Glass assured me that the English language was so richly creative that nothing I'd say would bring me harm! I might also invoke here the influence of that other strange mentor – Edward Lear – whose rhymes made so much sense to me that I have never been able to figure out why he called them *nonsense*.

CASE NARRATIVES

A Few Words

Almost every writer on matters creative and all trainers of creativity will tell you that nothing works like stories: stories are personal, real and telling. One of the most important things I had wanted to do the moment I began research for this book was to make a list of the people I would like to meet, talk to, observe and finally interview. From these activities have come the narratives — let's call them case narratives. Each of these wonderful people, who let me meet them and talk to them and interview them leads a rich, creative life. Their narratives will reveal much to the sensitive reader; embedded in their stories are valuable lessons for all of us who want to know something about the **magic** of creativity and what it does to people. These men and women are of different ages and come from markedly different backgrounds, cultures and countries. *All* are very successful. They are all very happy. They are all very creative and cling passionately to their creative selves. I hope you, my good reader, will share a little of the experience I had when I was in the presence of these glorious individuals. Though nothing can convey the complete experience of my meetings with them, I pray that the manner in which I represent them will enable some semblance of the joy to be felt. All of them were great, before, during and after the interviews and I want, once again, to express my profound thanks to them. All shortcomings here are mine — my creative people are there for us to learn from and bond with.

Verity Roennfeldt

The Lady Goes A—Bear-Ring

When I first met Verity she used to give me very very wet kisses. My word! You wouldn't have wanted to kiss another human being on earth – her kisses were so delectably engaging, wet and slurppy! That was in April 1976 and Verity was just about three years old. I was the guest of her parents at Ungarra, a small farming town some 80 kilometres away from the nearest big town called Tumby Bay, on South Australia's Eyre Peninsula. Ted Skewes, Verity's father, was then a board member of the Apex Club and had been assigned as my hospitality host. I recall taking a bus from Adelaide and riding in it for about seven hours before alighting at about 4.45 in the morning in cold, cold weather. And there was this tall, strong man ready to greet me.

Right from the start I knew I'd met a good man! Ted was a man after my own heart – a no-nonsense and straight-talking man. As soon as I was in his car (an old Volvo 144 – they don't make them like they used to!), he got talking and asked me the basic questions: what did I like, what didn't I eat, etc. So animated was our exchange that the long ride from Tumby Bay to Ungarra seemed like ten minutes! Ted was a farmer. (He was then managing a 2,300-acre farm, cultivating mainly wheat, but also clover and rearing cows and pigs and, as he used to remind me, a lot of hopeless stupid sheep and very, very annoying galas – birds which swept down and took every crumb of bread from your hands or simply delighted themselves by cawing away for hours and driving gentle farm folks like Ted nuts!) He'd given up his career as a surveyor for the Roads Department, married into a farming community and now had through sheer pluck and hard work made himself an important member of his community. On Ted's farm I met many interesting individuals, people who had never before seen a man with a turban. They wore hats all right, but didn't have the slightest clue as to what a turban was and who wore this "strange headgear"! The nearest they could associate me with was what Verity first uttered when she saw me: Ali Baba!

Ted and I are still the best of mates. Today he manages Pendleton Farm Retreat, a farm-stay resort owned by the Wesley Mission, designed to offer a pleasant getaway for individuals, families and groups desiring fresh air and to enrich their imagination through an intimate encounter with a green environment and different animals. Today Verity is a mother of three (so now it is her daughters who give me those wet kisses of yore!) and lives just outside one of Australia's more famous tourist attractions: the Great Ocean Road. Married to a wonderfully happy young man, Ben, who is hoping to become an academic researching fish habits, Verity today enjoys a lifestyle which would be the envy of many.

But this is Verity's story. And the underlying point of her story is that the people around her helped her realize just how creative she could be, and, indeed, is. "Right from the start," says Verity, "Dad and Mum just encouraged us (she and her sister Carmen) to roam the wheat fields, play with the cows and pigs and sheep, make our own toys and things. There was precious little we were not allowed to do. I grew up in a very **free** environment, always feeling brave and secure in my exploration of the wonderful world outside myself. I now realize, as you ask me these questions, Kirpal, that much of my creative instinct or ability, whatever you call it, came from those early childhood years. Especially the first three, four years, when I was the only child, really, around the house and enjoyed unlimited freedom of space, and even time."

I added, "I remember one of the first times I stayed for a long period with you guys was when it was the lambing season, and I was, I must confess, very surprised to see you helping your Dad in this: truly, when I saw your hand in the ewe trying to pull out the lamb, wow! That was quite something for a guy from Singapore!"

"Yes, from very young Dad taught me how to take out a lamb, and even, later, help pull out a calf who was stuck in the mother. That was so good, so beautiful – to help bring about a birth and recognize God's great beauty as it manifests itself all around us. I remember making a few mistakes and occasionally hurting the poor lamb or calf, but Dad was always there to reassure me and help me make a success of my task. I really think this support I received from both my parents was what gave me the strength, the courage, to do things, to be unafraid of venturing out, to giving birth, as it were, to new ideas."

Yes, today Verity is recognized as one of Australia's more creative personalities. She has created a special breed of bears for which the public, as it gets to hear and know about these special creations, is clamouring more and more. **Verity's work has been featured several times in *Australian Bear Creation's Magazine*, an influential and widely read craft magazine. One recent volume includes a detailed profile. She is known for her new and unique Merbears. I asked her to explain what these were.**

"Well," said Verity, holding her very special Merbear up and demonstrating its special features to me, "I was just sitting here one day, right here where we are facing our back garden but still inside the house, when an idea suddenly came to me: why should I carry on just making another teddy bear? I mean there are millions of teddy bears. Surely, I thought, there can be a new kind of bear. I rang Mum and shared this idea with her and she told me to go right ahead and make the first of a different kind of bear. I did.

When my husband came back from university that day, I proudly held my 'crude' creation up for inspection. And Ben smiled and gave me a hug and a kiss. And that's how the Merbears began their journey."

"How did the name come about?" I asked.

"I had, at this time, been writing some stories about humans and mermaids and things. So when I thought of a new bear, I just thought if there could be a mermaid, there could be a merbear! It was as simple as that! Merbears – bears that have a very special relationship with water (as normal bears don't) and who live on Merbear Island. Indeed, as I thought about this more and more, a whole new world emerged, stories just bursting to be told. The Merbear Kingdom opened up to me, and so there you are, Kirpal, my MerWorld – ready to be let loose upon the globe!"

I was mesmerized. Indeed, Verity has made dozens of Merbears, each with its unique character, physiology and face. Just before arriving for the interview with Verity I had rested at a beach hotel some hundred miles away from Verity's house and there, to my delight, I had found a Merbear on display: the hotelier, obviously, valued this new product and proudly exhibited it to his hotel guests! After the interview I checked out a couple more places where Verity's unique creations were on show. At another hotel in Adelaide as well as a clothes shop, the Merbear took its place among the many dolls. The Merbear – unique, unknown to the world but slowly coming into its own – is markedly different from the Sasha bears, the cuddly love bears. Here is a bear whose ties with humans are the core of hundreds of new creations – stories woven around a simple plot: the humans lose one of their children and the child is found and brought up by a Merbear – the rest is for readers to discover through reading Verity's books and eventually watching her movie, *Merworld*. Merbears also present and uphold many issues pertaining to the care of our world and the protection of our fragile environment. Merbears speak to adults and children alike, for we are never too young or old to learn – or to change our ways for the better.

I asked Verity to list the most significant factors which contributed to her sense of herself as a creative person. This is her list:

1. **Upbringing**. Vast, open spaces, life of a near-nomad, happy, green childhood, playing, wandering, exploring, helping Dad and Mum and being made to feel wanted as a helpmate. ("One thing you should mention, Kirpal, is that as a child I used to walk long hours by myself, wondering what was out there.")

2. **Bonding**. Establishing a good relationship with Dad and Mum and with others securing confidence, learning to share and feeling appreciated, realizing early that passing exams was not the only reason why I went to school. ("I once asked a teacher whether I could hand in a poem instead of an essay and, surprisingly the teacher replied, 'Why not?'")

3. **Reading and writing**. From very young I was encouraged to read a lot and write down what I felt about things and people. ("I even wrote about you and drew you as having a monkey face!") Mum always made me read what I had written and taught me how to use words. **I have found much affirmation and liberation of thought in keeping a journal.**

4. **Having the courage to take risks**. Be willing to venture out and try new things. Be unafraid of failure – it can only build your character. ("When I got married and Ben wanted to go to university, we had to make a major decision on **moving to another state with very little money. We decided to take the plunge, so to speak. This is how I could stay at home and create these bears, while also caring for our little ones.**")

5. **Making the most and best of things or people**. Using whatever help one can get, knowing the context one is in, asking for help (swallowing pride) and capitalizing on other people's strengths. ("My husband Ben's mother has a superb imagination and I **like to** ask her to share stories, narratives about her own life.")

Verity firmly believes in the efficacy of good communication and thinks creative people often lose out because of a lack of good communication skills. In her own life she has been through many a frustrating moment when people around her have not been able to convey what exactly it was they wanted, needed or desired. She says, "Whether it is personal – like husband to wife – or formal, like boss to employee, it is vital that we communicate with warmth and vitality. This is what I was taught from an early age, especially by Dad. And throughout my university career I lived by this philosophy and it has stood me well." Verity is not someone who suffers fools easily. "It is not that I am arrogant. Far from it," she says. "But people must also know that we do not live for their entertainment. I take serious people seriously and foolish people foolishly – it is just that the foolish ones don't last."

One way by which the so-called foolish people can last is to re-examine their inner selves and ask that old fundamental question: who am I? "It is when we begin to seek inside ourselves, go deep inside to ask basic questions, that our creative energies swell up. I believe most of us don't do this enough," says Verity. When I persisted in knowing more, Verity replied, "For example, many people don't want to acknowledge their source of inspiration; indeed, many don't even know they have or had a source of inspiration." "So what is your inspiration?" I ask. "God is my inspiration," Verity answers without flinching.

I point out that behind much of what she said and did was an almost sacramental approach to time. "Yes," says Verity, "yes, time is of the essence. Because we don't have forever, we have to make the most of now ... this is what drives me ... this urgency is what makes me do all these (pointing to her kids, her merbears, her manuscripts) ... and I think all creative people share this thing about time and timing."

In the course of the long interview, Verity and I discussed so many different aspects of creativity. But again and again one note struck a big, big chord: courage to be different. "I breast-fed my kids, as you know. This, well – having kids – means constant round the clock work – including housework and all that is seemingly mundane. But I welcome this 'burden' or 'calling' namely 'parenthood' because, like breast-feeding is a physical bond – routine and duty bonds me spiritually and mentally to my babies. The 'mundane-ness' of 'duties' is transformed daily as I find new ways to be different and more time efficient. Likewise, my creativity, my creations, as for my babies – I give them the best I have."

True to what she has said, Verity pays utmost attention to every little detail of every Merbear she makes and crafts. And when she writes those wonderful narratives about the fascinating characters who people her Merbear Kingdom, each minute aspect is given emphasis. When her big story, weaving the different strands of so many tiny ones, is made into the movie, *Merworld*, we viewers can expect Verity's fastidiousness to show. Here is one creator who takes her every creation very seriously.

Feng Da Hsuan

Atomizer and Professor Extraordinaire

When one first enters Professor Feng Da Hsuan's sparsely decorated office at the University of Texas in Dallas where he is currently Vice-President of Research and Graduate Education, one is immediately struck by the fact that several ties and a few jackets are easily seen. The roving eye then takes in several black-and-white photographs hanging on the walls, some coloured ones and a family photo on his workdesk. Da Hsuan's workspace is huge. I teased him about this, saying, "Wow! This is enough for both you and me plus at least ten others!" To which he crisply responded, "Now you know why!". And huge, too, is his current portfolio. In between sips of Chinese tea (which he insists is any time better than the combined ingredients of all the different colas!) he tells me, "I believe, if you ask me, that the real reason UTD hired me is that they want me to use my extensive network to build a real, progressive, international research culture here." The stress is on **international** because for too long UTD had tended to be rather inward-looking. The new millennium was bringing in new demands, new expectations, new scenarios and if an academic institution wanted to maintain its excellence and move forward, especially in terms of research, it had to look for people who are very well-connected outside of the US. Of course Da Hsuan fitted the bill perfectly!

Both Da Hsuan's parents were from China. His father was a newspaper man, essentially an editor, quite effectively bilingual in Chinese and English – as the illustrious son is now. His mother was a musician who played classical instruments, both Chinese and Western. But she especially loved the violin and the piano and for years was acclaimed as one of the finest piano and violin teachers. "So did your own creative urges come from your parents?" I ask.

Da Hsuan pauses, looks at me somewhat sharply and replies, "You mean whether my parents taught me creativity?"

"No," I clarify, "but whether by their own example they gave you inspiration and also provided space for creative dreaming ..." I do not get to finish the statement because Da Hsuan is already in a reflective, almost contemplative mood, and is telling me, "Yes, yes, both Mum and Dad, but more Mum. Yes, Mum always encouraged me to dream. She'd sit with me and ask me loads of questions which usually had very little to do with my schoolwork, but more with how my day had been, the special things I had done or had wanted to do and so on. I suppose you could say that yes, my parents influenced me one heck of a lot ... I don't usually think about this but now that you mention it, yes, my parents taught me a lot. I owe them more than just my education, I owe them also my drive, my goal-aspiring attitude." He gently takes hold of my shoulder, turns me around and says, "Do you see these Chinese calligraphic scrolls? They are very significant to me. They basically say, **hard work comes only to those who inspire and lead, but they are amply rewarded**. My parents taught me not to be afraid of glass ceilings, saying most ceilings were glass ceilings."

In another part of the office are other wall-hangings – portraits, signed photographs, certificates, tokens of appreciation, gift-paintings and the like – Da Hsuan is sentimental, though he takes great pains to hide this. One photograph shows him as a cowboy, hat and all, riding a horse. "Do you pretend a lot?" I ask. Again he ponders. Then with a somewhat quizzical smile he responds, "In Physics you have something known as the **error-bar** – yes, I pretended I could go beyond this artificially treated **error-bar**." He then patiently explains to me the various integers, variables, configurations, square root of -1, structure of molecules, "stripping reactors", the juxtapositioning of nuclear physics with mathematics, how protons, neutrons and other "ons" synergize, particularly when one is theorizing about the construction of bridges! I listen in rapt attention. But I am hungry for more in respect of his amazing intellectual prowess. After all, here is a man who had distinguished himself from a young age, had authored and edited more than 20 books and over 190 scientific and professional articles in some of the world's most highly respected journals. "Right from the start," he tells me, "I used to say, 'Maybe I can do that ...' "

"I used to listen to my mother playing the piano and my mind would wander. Memory now plays tricks but I recall that often I thought about combining art, dance, maths and physics, subjects I enjoyed. In some ways my childhood expectations were unreal. My dean at the University of Minnesota was a kind, gentle man, with the usual rigour associated with the best of Jewish intellectuals. He probably taught me most about what you are interested in: creativity. **Asking questions actively** – that's what creativity requires you to do. If you ask mechanical questions you get mechanical solutions ... intuition must be involved if one is to be even remotely close to the cutting edge. I learnt a lot from my meetings with this scholarly man. My PhD years were among the most boundary-breaking." I venture a question: "Since you had your primary and secondary education in Singapore, would you say that where Singapore is lagging today is in its inability to intuit?" "Not so simple," replies Da Hsuan, "no, no, that would be simplifying the whole system. No, but you must remember, it takes a total change of culture for an educational system to value creativity. And even then you can never be sure that the students are going to prove creative. In any case, what **is** creativity? For the Chinese, for many Chinese, creativity spells trouble, you know, because it allows the unknown to enter and participate in one's life, one's method." "But isn't this precisely why you are different?" I ask. "Yes, but, no ... err, well, yes and no. Look, read this," says Da Hsuan, pointing to yet another of those on-the-wall thingys. "**No trespassers: violators will be shot, survivors will be shot again**!" I can't help but laugh. He too laughs. He went on, "I knew you'd enjoy that. You see, science, especially physics, maths, these are **difficult** subjects and Singapore's education system has so far been excellent in training students in these disciplines. But you need more, you need that extra **oomph**, that sense of wonder, of knowing you matter."

We talk about and discuss various movements and theories in physics. Da Hsuan is an acknowledged authority in a number of highly technical areas: mathematical physics, quantum physics, nuclear physics, nuclear astrophysics (now that's one to bewilder ordinary chaps like me!), quantum optics. Trying to be clever, I raise a question: "I have always believed that quarks were fictional." He looks at me, laughs and says, "Kirpal, I marvel at you. I thought you were mainly a literature person. I have enjoyed reading your work, but quarks … well, that takes us somewhere else!" Of course I didn't dare pursue this; but he continued, "Here at UTD we are big, *big* in nanotechnology – you know, the technology of minute things. This is all about breaking molecules up so that theoretically you could walk through walls, as at incredibly high speeds matter will dissolve, penetrate solid structures and reconstitute itself on the other side." I am mesmerized. "Really? You mean David Copperfield could be true?" Again he laughs. "I think it is going to be hard for you to fathom the fundamental changes which are coming about in this very intricate field. We are on the cutting edge here. And my role mainly is to bring in people, like MacDiarmid, the Nobel laureate, to make sure that UTD stays on top of things. In science, progress can be phenomenal, exponential, and there is no time to stand and stare. Unlike your field, literature, in physics, things are today getting enormously exciting – as we explore the frontiers of space, our own frontiers beckon exploration, and here is where a new synthesis is going to happen … we are going to witness a transition unknown to man."

Basically, for the past eight years or so, Da Hsuan has been more an administrator than a researcher ("Not quite true," he tells me, "I told the President of UTD I *must* keep my research … and I have been allowed to do this"). At Drexel University where at an early age he became the W. Russell Weber Chair Professor of Physics, Da Hsuan was given leave-of-absence to be Director of HUBS (Hospitals, Universities, Businesses, Schools) – a unique scheme to bring together the different arms of the community so as to propel research to bring about a more exciting, educationally rich environment. Da Hsuan was Vice-President of HUBS from 1998 to 2000. Concurrently he was General Manager of SAIC (Science Applications for International Corporations). HUBS and SAIC were big, multi-million dollar programmes. Both are still running today and he remains intimately involved with them. The many years of highly intensive research at some of the world's foremost laboratories (Los Alamos, Brookhaven National Laboratory, Oak Ridge, the Niels Bohr Institute, Max Planck Institute, among others) obviously left their mark on this seeker of scientific truth. "Life is full of opportunities," Da Hsuan tells me, "it is often what we make of these…" I could not agree more.

So I ask him, "How is it that you have been so successful not only in doing so much but with such ease?" "I have been very, very lucky, frankly," he says. "You see, it is like this. In the course of my work in astrophysics, I got to know Congressman Curt Welden. We got on like a house on fire. He helped open new doors and windows. I have never liked the idea of being a cocoon professor – many science profs are cocoons – so every time an opportunity to move outside of academia came, I grabbed it. But I always had my fallback position at the university. The way I see it, there must always be **security** if one is to be creative; a creative leap can only happen when one works, dreams in security, not without it." This is of great interest to me because many creative people have been reckless, to say the least. "Maybe, maybe," Da Hsuan concedes, "but I think nowadays it would be hard for anyone to be creative and reckless, the world is just too complex. You know Einstein said, "The true laws of nature cannot be linear nor can they be derived from such." I feel the same way about creativity: it is no longer just enough to dream … we need to work and work and work, otherwise dreams will remain just that, dreams."

Was this an apposite place for me to conclude our formal interview? No, though his lovely secretary had come in several times to remind him of important appointments and to get his signature on documents I decided there were two more questions I wanted to ask. First, what did he make of the phrase "**thinking out of the box**"? "Well," says Da Hsuan, "Curt Welden is, essentially, a politician. Most people would have said politics and good scholarship don't mix, or don't mix well. But I thought otherwise. Here was a good-natured man wanting to help the academia grow in new and adventurous ways. Why not? Could we achieve a good, healthy balance of politics and scholarship? Yes ... now that is one way of answering your question."

Okay. Second, when, for him, had the creative urge been the most crucial? "When I became an Assistant Professor at Drexel," he replied. "You see, when you are a graduate student, there's always your supervisor to help you, and the other fellow students also help. But when you get your first university appointment, well, then you are on your own. The senior ones have little or no time for you; those at your level are all competing for tenure, kudos, etc. That, for me, was when I had to think of creative ways of teaching, researching, publishing, experimenting, even living ..." I cut in, "Well you obviously have succeeded in all these areas. You have a wife, a daughter and a son." "Yes," he responds, calmly, quietly, "but it has not always been easy."

Here I thought was a good moment to stop. I thanked him for his invaluable time, noting that here was an academic who had had the courage and the vision to go beyond the pale of ordinary professorial life and getting things done. No wonder he had been awarded so many honours, including six honorary professorships in China alone. For UTD Professor Feng Da Hsuan is building a momentous relationship of dedicated individuals, all wanting to do just that little bit more to ensure a safer environment for us all. Da Hsuan's experience both within academia and outside it stands him in absolute good stead. As do the little teachings of his mother as she sang him to sleep. Later, over dinner, I could see his eyes getting moist as he reminisced. Though his parents are not around now to see the wonderful achievements of their glorious son, the rest of the world takes notice. Even as I conclude this, Da Hsuan has just been given another award, the Inside Collin County 21 for 21, for his entrepreneurship, vision and above all, his commitment and passion for creating a viable and creative university research culture which warmly embraces all who show a serious desire to be different, new and of **this** millennium. This is rare, especially in universities, most of which continue to exist in their isolated bliss of ivory towers in Jurassic parks.

Alejandro Fogel

Recreating Footsteps and Pioneering Art Forms

Meeting Alejandro Fogel for the first time can be an interesting experience: apart from his ponytail, which he always keeps neat and tidy. He is your typical Latino – charming, handsomely chiselled (the muscles show right through the thin clothes he wears!) and soft-spoken. I first met Alejandro in 1997 in Iowa City. He lived in a beautiful suburban house and at the time I first met him, he was giving a party mainly to the writers from the Latin-American countries who were part of my International Writing Programme. He introduced us to *mate*, the typical Argentinian tea that we had to sip from a small container. The entire tea-making and tea-drinking process was a ritual. I enjoyed it very much though in itself the tea did not taste too different from the many I had already sampled during my travels around the world.

Men and women both find Alejandro extremely attractive. When I met him for this interview – in August 2002 in New York City where he now lives – I made it a point to ask him, "What do you feel about being so attractive?" He replies, "For me, attraction is almost something innate; you either have it or you don't. I seem to have been very lucky – (laughing) maybe it's the genes? But to be serious, I think we could all become attractive if we took time and energy to look more inside ourselves. I believe people who look **inside** become more attractive than those who don't." To me this is a somewhat strange theory. He looks at my puzzled face and continues, "You see, Kirpal, most people don't want to know themselves, but it is through knowing ourselves that we become attractive. Real attractiveness is an **inner** quality which some of us seem to have because we look deep down inside ourselves. I have always looked inside myself. My father especially taught me this, and it is this looking inside which has given me the strength to live and survive in a not-so-very-nice world."

Alejandro urges me to have the lovely mocha and the rich chocolate cake he has bought for both of us in a side-street café in bustling New York City. It is morning and most people seem to be going about their business, indifferent to the two of us trying to discuss the nature of attraction and its relationship to creativity. I reflect on how Alejandro's father fled his home in Romania to escape the Holocaust, how Alejandro was born in Argentina and how from a very young age this gifted artist grew up with the strong urge and sense to set the record straight about his father's life, his father's big escape from the clutches of Nazi Germany and now his own coming to terms with some of life's major questions. I think about the many different roads and routes Alejandro has travelled to get here: from learning English (he grew up speaking Spanish) to changing his own profile from being, simply, a painter to a multimedia artist, now in 2002 specializing in making short, intense films (docu-fiction) and computer art. I think about the numerous awards and fellowships this fascinating man has won and the many museums and galleries (both private and public) which house and exhibit his works. I think of the many countries he has visited and taught – the US (which is now home), Canada, Australia, Germany, France, Israel, the UK, Belgium – just to mention a few. I think.

Alejandro senses my reflective mood and says, "You asked me earlier to think about my **creative self**. Let me put it this way. My creative work is my whole life, and my whole life is part of my creative work. I cannot divorce my life from my work. I will die if I did that. Every second I live, every breath I take is, for me, creative. I need, I must do something creative or else life becomes meaningless. Most of my work is autobiographical. It relies on **memory**, and I believe all memories are inside us. We need to bring them up; we need to bring them to the surface so that we can express them in our creative works. This is why I say creativity cannot always be targeted; often it is free, spontaneous. Once we have expressed ourselves, once the memories have surfaced and come out, then, ah, then we might be able to target, as it were, our end works. This may sound pompous, but I feel compelled by the collective unconscious – from images and symbols in literature and painting to the stories of my father's generation. From the age of about 13–14 years I have been different; everyone around me told me so too. Yes, and since then I have been writing poems, stories, histories, whatever, I have also been just drawing, painting, making things, making people and objects come alive. This is what creativity is: seeing life around us and making this life real."

I am overwhelmed. Collective unconscious? I thought I had left Jung far, far behind. But no, here was a contemporary Jungian, a firm believer in the power of art to transform the human psyche. I look at him searchingly and ask, "So how would you define creativity?" He answers, "For me creativity is exploration, nothing short of the exploration of the cosmos. I look at the blue sky, I look at my canvas, I look at my computer screen and I explore how all three can be connected. And they are. They become connected, linked, through the strange, almost mystical, power of the cosmos, the cosmic energy. (Here, I should tell the reader, Alejandro's eyes become fiery. Looking at him, I am reminded a little of the ancient mariner, fiercely absorbed in his own world of the collective unconscious as Alejandro is telling me of his life's vision.) "Look at this, Kirpal," he adds, "look, look at my hand. See the lines, see the way in which these lines connect, lead? It is the same, if we look, if we look with our inner eyes we can find connections everywhere. The cosmos, the cosmos is huge and we are small, but we become huge, too, in recognizing this special link between each of us and the great cosmic energy which keeps the universe going."

All of this is too much for me. I slowly drink my mocha and eat the rich chocolate cake. But Alejandro is not finished; he continues, "I cannot stand and simply don't like coincidences. So many times people, even artists, say, 'Oh, this is all because of a coincidence, a strange coincidence …' Coincidence, my foot! There are *no* coincidences − everything is destined, predetermined, ordered, patterned … we just need to establish the links, find their meanings. Often these are revealed to us in symbols and images. If we know where to look we know how to find them. This is why we can only live in the present, the immediate present. I live now, now." "But," I interject, "you said just now that we need memory, memory is of the past …" "No," he replies. "Who says memory is of the past? No, of course not! My memory is here, with me, right here, right now. This is what I was trying to tell you − we look inside and bring the memory up. So now is the only memory we consciously know and grasp. So we train ourselves to discover the other memories within us. We meditate, we take long walks, we sit silently listening to the sounds of the night lights, we hear the colours of the blue sky, we feel the cadences of the myths which our grandmothers told us … yes, we do all of these and all of everything makes us want to create."

I interrupt and ask him to tell me something about his education. "Education?" asks Alejandro. "Well, it was pretty normal, I should say. But as I told you, from secondary school they found me to be different from the other boys and often they used to leave me alone. So I was left alone and this gave me a chance to live in my own world of thoughts and imagination." "Ah huh," I say. "That's it − Imagination! Now **that** is what I think is crucial to creativity." "Yes," says Alejandro, "Yes. But you cannot ignore the role of memory. Because if you don't allow memory to play with your imagination, you have nothing. Or rather what you will have is mainly the stuff of existence, not living. And good creative works don't result from existence; they are the result of living, of life!" (Alejandro again becomes very passionate in his speech so that people around us, I notice surreptitiously, are looking in our direction, perhaps wondering at the pitch of our conversation.) "Life is beautiful if we make it so, Kirpal. It is. So you take 9/11 – yes, you visited Ground Zero yesterday. What does it tell you? What does it show you? What does it do to you? What does it make you feel? You see people around, some crying, some lost, some just curious, some unsure, some, like you, awed, saddened … yes, all of these. But 9/11 … think of the memory, think of what it will mean for years and years to come. You cannot forget memory, Kirpal. 9/11 was not a coincidence. We have to find out more about the truth behind 9/11. And believe me the creative people will. And we will then write stories, make theatre, draw paintings. 9/11 will be art, reaching out to the cosmos …"

At this point, just next to us, a perambulator with a baby inside has somehow toppled to one side. Before we can help, the mother of the baby has rushed to it and all is once again normal. "You see what just took place? If the mother was not driven by an inner force she would have taken her time to come and set the perambulator straight. The baby inside is the woman's link to her memory. Like her we are all connected through memory. Nothing is the result of coincidence." Obviously my friend Alejandro has a thing about coincidence. So I ask, "Why are you so bothered by this coincidence thing?" "Why, you ask me why?" he replies. "I'll tell you why. Whenever something very bad happens, people say it must be coincidence. Bullshit. Think about the Holocaust – was that a coincidence? Was it a coincidence that Hitler became what he became – a monster? No, Kirpal, no. We must never hide behind rationalizations. Coincidence is a rationalization for the weak-hearted, for those who don't want to accept the tragedy and truth of reality. Likewise 9/11 is not a coincidence. Somebody somewhere meant it to be and it has become. Hitler might not have become what he did if that art academy had admitted him."

We discuss politics now. And history. For Alejandro one big mistake the modern educational system has made is that it has not emphasized enough the learning of history through literature. Recorded history, the history written by historians, is seldom interesting or engaging because it is dry, containing facts and figures. But history as told through the eyes of the writers, poets, painters and the cartoonists even (and Alejandro tells me he loves good cartoons), now history presented this way is engaging and interesting. But is such history not subjective? Prejudiced? Of course it is. But everything is subjective, says Alejandro, we are all subjective. But if this is so, I say, then creativity, because it is subjective, cannot appeal to many people. Also, if creativity is subjective, then why should we buy your art?

I know I have got Alejandro worked up again. To see him get worked up is in itself a wonderful experience. Because he is such a gentle human being. When we meet and he hugs me, I feel always the hug of a strong man gently welcoming me into his world. "You know I don't like cheap art. Cheap art is that which panders. Propaganda. There was a lot, a lot of cheap art during the Holocaust. And the great art, the real art was stolen, destroyed and burnt. This is why the history of the Holocaust, the real history, is still being written after all these years, and painted. And made into film. I am also recording the real history of the Holocaust, the history which the so-called historians will never know and therefore never write about. My father, for instance, his family. Yes, each and every human being who went through that hell has a real story to tell and it is this telling which challenges us artists. Can we, as artists, ever capture Truth? Can our art ever be adequate to the truth of history, the truth of memory? I doubt it, this is why the world's best anything has yet to be created. So long as we live, so long will we keep trying to create the best poem, the best story, the best film, the best painting ... I don't know, Kirpal, life is short and art is long as someone said, but we keep at it, we keep trying. Like you, you try and write the history of your family, your country, your daughters. Like you, so many of us do the same. Is creativity therefore not worth buying? Certainly to those for whom it has no value, it is not worth buying. But there is no true price tag to a creative work. And never, never will anyone be able to price the process behind that creative work, the finished product. It is, for me, the process which is crucial. And if my works are expensive, as some people tell me they are – *you* tell me they are (we laugh) – it is because you are paying for the process, that search for the inner memory."

It is now past lunchtime. We have been sitting and talking for more than four hours. As the crowd slowly walks by, we decide it is time for us to move too. I ask him one last question, "Alejandro, my friend, tell me – can creativity flourish if we don't teach people how to value it?" "Yes and no," replies Alejandro. "Creativity will flourish wherever it is because real creativity does not need people to value it; it is its own best value. But, yes, I can see where you are coming from. If we don't educate people, then people will not know the value of creativity. And then we will all be very poor. No one will come to your poetry readings or buy your poems, and no one will come to my art exhibitions or buy my paintings, my films." We laugh.

Shelley Berc

Shaping Wilderness and Spreading Good

I watch her sitting almost curled on her white sofa. The apartment is right in the heart of Manhattan. Outside the view is extraordinarily clear – the sky is vivid blue and all the skyscrapers are identifiable. "Isn't it lovely outside?" she asks. "Of course," I reply, "but you are lovelier!" "You old charmer, you!" she exclaims. "Come and sit here and tell me what you think of my story."

What do I think? Me? Well, if I had thought any less of her, this wonderfully gentle woman would not be in this book. Our first meeting was a pure coincidence. August, 1997, Iowa. I was in Iowa as Distinguished International Writer in their world-famous International Writing Programme and Shelley Berc was the Professor of Drama. She was associated with the IWP because through her numerous connections writers were able to have their works performed, or at least dramatized, around the US. Thus, for example, I had my poems dramatized in Maine by the Portland Stage Company, as well as in New York, off Broadway, by the well-known New York Theatre Workshop (the company responsible for the original "Rent").

We met one evening, quite by chance. "Aren't you the guy from Singapore?" she asked, sidling up to me along the corridor of the famous Mayflower apartments where the IWP writers were housed. "Yes," I answered, "and who, pray is the beautiful you?" And so began a relationship which can best be described as "unique". Since that autumn evening in Iowa City Shelley and I have remained and become almost like family. I say "almost" because if we define family as a unit which knows everything about itself, then I have to confess that there are so many sides and aspects of Shelley which I don't know. Indeed, I wonder whether anyone knows her at all? Her small, frail form beguiles; she is tough. "When you have to compete in a family given to intense achievement, you have to be tough – it's the only way to survive," she says. I ask "Really?" "Yes, my sister and I competed in and about literally everything. Of course she won! Look – this is her apartment; isn't it gorgeous?" The apartment is gorgeous; as we speak, the sound of cars becomes more audible. "Come," she says invitingly, "let's go to the corner and talk over some real, good coffee."

At the corner café (which appears to be a *habitué* of hers) Shelley relaxes after waiting in the queue for 15 minutes, insisting that I sit down and just wait for her and our cups of coffee. "New York City is impossible!" she says. "I hate it and love it, as do most of us New Yorkers. But you know what? I could not live anywhere else – not even in your clean, green and safe Singapore." I have my cue: "Do you think safety is necessary for creativity?" I ask, perhaps a little too pointedly because Shelley looks down through her big glasses and starts to sip her coffee. I wait for her to speak; over the years I have gotten to know that she has this habit of ignoring, so to speak, a pertinent issue before confronting it. "Are we safe, Kirpal?" she asks. "Are we ever safe? From hurt? From love? From pain? No, I don't think so. I don't think safety is essential for creativity. Sometimes it is fear which begets creativity. Like they say, 'Necessity is the mother of invention.'" "Yes, see. Invention," I interrupt, "but we are talking about creativity, not invention." My intrusion seems to have jarred her train of thought. She continues, "I thought I was safe, very safe, once, but now I just live from one day to the next, believing that anything could happen." It is, after all, post-9/11. "You see, Kirpal, for me creativity is the joyful making of something which is not there, like out there, but within myself. And I have this need, this great urge, to bring it out of myself. In creativity, I am like a child; I need my privacy, my space, my freedom. So, yes, maybe in a sense, safety is required, but more the safety of 'thought'. I was very shy as a child, I'm still shy but survival made me strong. I used to go out and talk to flowers – I'd tell them stories, read them poems I had composed. I think we need safety from politics and the politicians. If I had been a lawyer, say from Yale, I'd have been a very different person today. My grandmother pushed us and pushed us, and I have always remembered my grandmother as a demanding woman. I find my safety in love these days. Also my creativity. Without love, peace, quiet, serenity, I don't think I can write or create anything. I have always needed someone to love my vision. Now I have this. In a sense I am safe."

I am not sure if this continuous outpouring of deeply felt emotion is where I truly want to go in my discussion about creativity with this gifted and extremely talented writer. Shelley Berc, whose play I had just watched on Broadway (*The New York Times* had not, I thought, been totally fair in its review of the play but what the heck! – it made it to its pages!); Shelley Berc who had won so many research awards and grants that she could be the envy of us all. Was it her 'Judaic' background which made her what she is today? "Yes and no," she says, "because backgrounds lose their significance when the adult enters the playing field." She talks in theatrical terms – her life is a stage, constructed chiefly by her now and on this stage a play is being enacted with her being its director as well as its creator. Shelley is the playwright-adaptor *par excellence*; for her creativity resides in taking what is there and remaking it beyond belief!

She continues, "You know, my parents were both quite creative in their own way; they found ways of escaping the reality around them. I think that is creative! I, too, am an escapist, I escape into my work, my plays, my fiction ... even my cats!" I stop her here: cats and I don't always get along (I want to make a naughty pun but I know this is not the right time). I shift the line of questioning. "Why did you call your novel *The Shape of Wilderness*?" I ask. Though primarily a playwright, Shelley had this strange first novel to her name, a complex weaving of near-tragic narratives. "Funny you should ask that – I don't know the answer myself. It just came to me one day as I was thinking about my second novel. Do you like the two main characters in the novel? They are intertwined almost by fate ... maybe that is why there is the shape of wilderness. It took me several years to finish that book, perhaps it was too close to call. But everybody I know writes the 'virgin' book and following that, there is much pain. Maybe I ought not to have written it?" I can see near-tears in her eyes; she does not look too happy being asked about this novel.

Suddenly she says, "At the Yale Drama School, I was very lucky. I had very good instructors, teachers who took a real interest in my writing, my work. Now I think that is important for creativity: caring and attention. I got both. You know drama is an odd choice for creative expression. When you devise a play, or write a play, you don't just create characters, you create, primarily conflict, conflict without which the characters have nothing much to do. You remember Forster's category of flat and round characters? No character can be flat on stage, not even the one who only has one line or the one who just walks across the stage without saying anything." Shelley is intent on talking now. I know she has a lot more to say about this interface between creativity and creator. "When I create characters or when I rewrite characters from history, I reflect on their private inner space. I 'connect' with them, sometimes I become them ... how can I know them enough otherwise to put them on stage, exhibit them, subject them to the scrutiny of my audiences?" "Do you worry about what your audience say or think?" I ask. "Of course," she replies. "I create to bring joy, inner joy; I want my audience to see the life of characters from a perspective which they have not had the benefit of doing before. I demand a lot from my audience just as I demand a lot from myself. I cannot suffer fools. I am sorry, Kirpal, call me a snob, but I demand that my audience listens, listens with the inner heart to what I am telling them." "Your plays almost always carry a message – there is always an agenda," I point out. "No safety there," she chuckles.

Shelley studied at Amherst College. So, naturally I ask her about Emily Dickinson. "Now, there you have a genuine talent, a real creative spirit," she says. Spirit? "Yes, her spirit is still there in the trees surrounding her house. I spent a lot of time just wandering around there, reflecting on her poems. Dark and brooding, she was sick mostly, but what a way with words!

Since I could not stop for Death/Death stopped for me.

Was she morbid as most critics say? I don't think so. She lived and wrote what she felt – that is *not* morbidity, but adherence to truth. The true creative artist upholds truth no matter what. And she was a true, original and great artist." It does not matter in the least whether Shelley had quoted the lines correctly; I am taken in by the intensity of Shelley's convictions about truth and creativity. To her, it is abundantly clear, creativity cannot be divorced from passionate conviction; values count; attitudes matter very much. "When I was a child, I used to hear 'whisperings'... I don't know where they came from, but these whisperings stimulated my mind, gave my imagination wild ideas to play with. I sometimes wonder if it was the same for Emily."

As the clock moves towards the noon hour, when hundreds would flock to the café we were at for their quick lunch, I made another attempt at making Shelley articulate her concept of creativity. She too sensed that time was running away from us. "You ask difficult and awkward questions, Kirpal. Truly we should talk about these sensitive, never-to-be-fully-answered questions at length. You cannot expect me to answer you right away. But I know you want me to say something for this bloody book of yours. Okay, think. Put it this way. For too long creativity has been seen as an individual act, a one-person activity. For me the lustre of that definition, that understanding of creativity, no longer attracts. I believe most deeply that all creativity *is* a collaborative act and nowhere do you see this more evidently than in theatre, in the creation of plays. This is what I do. I collaborate. I collaborate creatively. When I ask my creativity workshop participants (and you know this, you were there with us in Samos) to do 'automatic drawing', that is collaborative creativity because it builds upon the forces which are altogether there. There is 'collective energizing' … *that* is creativity. Some day I hope to demonstrate more powerfully what I mean. Take the sun and solar energy, for instance. Look, see, as soon as you think about this one word, this one image, you become involved in an entire series of symbols and images, maybe even myths and legends. There is a kind of 'cosmic' serendipity; something that might approximate all the *plexuses* which poor old D. H. Lawrence was trying so hard to sell to us. I could simply say, 'Creativity is my story of this planet'. You will get a definition, the kind your scholar critics will like. But no, that is not what creativity truly is. Creativity is much, much bigger than all the definitions found in dictionaries, bigger than you and me, bigger than this entire universe." I realized Shelley had begun to wax lyrical, as they say. Sitting there, completely oblivious of the couple standing over us and watching us, wanting us to get up and leave the seats to them, I was enraptured. Shelley is so beautiful when she is like this; her intellect is formidable, her spirit thirsty. "If we don't have colour in the world," she carries on, "the world will go away. That is what creativity is: colour, brilliant and captivating, it adds to our humdrum existence; it makes our living rich and bearable; it gives us freshness; it makes us new. Creativity is a mystery, like our planet, like you, like me, like all of us."

I leave it there. As we walk back to her apartment, the taxis on the road sound their horn while the clouds overhead get a little duller. Shelley puts her lovely arm around my shoulder and says, "Kirpal, in the end we don't know what creativity is. Admit it!"

Ong Keng Sen
Creatively Defying Expectations

Many years ago, when Ong Keng Sen had just hit the Singapore theatre scene, a friend told me that this *enfant terrible* was going to prove to be like that crazy woman Caroline Lamb chasing Byron, "mad, bad and dangerous". Whether it was the lady or Byron to whom these words referred do not matter much; what mattered was my friend's conviction that this new smart-ass of the Singapore stage was not going to be easy to deal with. Well, interestingly enough, the years seem to have proven my friend right. For Keng Sen has done mad things; to many he's been bad and to a few he's even been dangerous! Naturally all of these terms are used advisedly, because while conferring on this extremely provocative but delightfully creative director/dramaturge a certain definite notoriety, they also do suggest that there is a lot of fondness and affection for him even from his most vociferous detractors. As another friend put it, how can anyone find Keng Sen irritating, even if they do find him offensive?

"There was nothing unusual in my upbringing, Kirpal," Keng Sen tells me. "In fact, it was a very ordinary upbringing – you know, average Chinese family – very Chinese, mind you, trying to make sure their son went to university, did well and brought honour and fame." Half-serious and half-cheeky, Keng Sen talks to me about his childhood and university days (when he really began to be earnest about theatre) in the spare room of his TheatreWorks (the professional theatre company of which Keng Sen is the Artistic Director) workspace at the beautiful historic site of Fort Canning in Singapore. Around us lie posters, newspapers, magazines, videos, CD-ROMs, VCDs, DVDs, some odd props, costumes and photographs. He has just returned from Europe, and one of the more memorable things he's done this time around (it is end-November 2002) is to produce "Hamlet" in the old Kronberg Castle. "No, I don't think my parents were aware of something we now call **creativity**, no, not at all. What they did know is that people who sang and danced and acted were not exactly what they'd call 'properly educated'." "So were you 'properly educated'?" I ask. "Yes and no," replies Keng Sen. "At first they were very proud of me – I guess they still are, especially my mother – and when I started working in the lawyer's office and started to bring some money back every month, they were pleased, visibly pleased. In the meantime, of course, I had started to show a lot of interest in theatre. I started to return home late and also to show less and less keenness in my office work. It was hard at first, trying to make my family believe that my calling, as it were, was not in law but in theatre…"

Was it difficult to leave the cushy job of a lawyer, especially in Singapore where a successful lawyer can earn more than US$1million a year after about ten years' practice? "Yes," Keng Sen replies. "From one point of view I'd agree that I could have become a successful lawyer in the terms you have just described, but was that what I really wanted? Money? No. For me, being fulfilled inside matters more, much, much more. In fact, now that I think about it, it has always been this way for me, even from when I was little I had always wanted to do my thing, get my way, whether it was a little toy or whether it was carrying my dirty little sleep-pillow around with me – you know, the kind of **security-comfort** thingy? I now think I have always been a kind of spoilt child, wanting my own way. It was only after graduating that I began to fully understand this part of myself." "And now that you understand this part, would you say that for the creative person there is **no** compromise?" I ask. "That, Kirpal, is a very hard question to answer," said Keng Sen. "You know, at first it was always compromise, compromise and compromise. Because in TheatreWorks we were always short of funds, money was a *big* thing. No money, no show. No show, no go! So, yes, I had to battle a lot of people, from my colleagues within TheatreWorks to people outside it. So yes, I feel I did compromise my creativity. I imagine many creative artists have to do likewise."

Keng Sen is fired now, I can see it in his eyes; suddenly they are bright, even in the dimness of the room we are sitting in. He is visibly agitated, his legs fly out in two opposite directions, nearly kicking me off my seat ("Sorry!" he says), his arms gesticulate and he carries on, "But you know when I had had about 5–6 years doing this (compromising) I decided enough was enough. So I started to put my foot down more and more. Call it arrogance, call it artistic temperament, but people around me began to notice that I was not going to be easily pushed around especially when it came to what I considered major and important artistic, creative decisions." "Like what, for example?" I ask. "Well, like wanting to use that huge fountain in Suntec City for a performance – you remember, you were there? That was the first time such a thing had ever happened. Right there, in the middle of Singapore's bustling prosperity, where the financial types made their millions, right there I was staging a play designed to question Singapore's materialism, Singapore's blind adherence to a pragmatic philosophy." Of course I remember this – how could anyone forget? The whole experience was mind-boggling; people were literally taken on a kind of **theatre-tour**, moving in groups from one performance space to another, all ending up around the biggest fountain in Asia, watching actors struggle in tanks of water as if water represented a kind of perverse suffocation. Audience reactions, like everything that Keng Sen has done, was mixed; some loved it, some questioned it, and some didn't know what to make of it.

"Does the fact that many who see your shows don't understand what you are trying to do bother you?" I ask. "Of course it does!" says Keng Sen. "Doesn't it bother you when people say, 'Kirpal, I don't understand what your poems are about'? Of course. But one perseveres; one keeps trying to make them see. More significantly, trying to make them feel. You remember those plays we put on in our Black Box (a theatre)? Many had political or sexual themes; well, people bought tickets, sat and watched in silence and then went home mostly wondering what the hell we were up to. Tay Tong (Keng Sen's artistic partner) would say to me, 'You know they call up and say we are avant-garde, we are too experimental, they want normal theatre, they just want good entertainment.' So okay, we decided we would cater to different audiences with different performances. But I always knew where my real creative energies were going to be – in new, totally different kinds of theatre experiences. Yes, totally new!"

It is hard to refute this. From the start Keng Sen's artistic direction has been nothing short of **different**. I recall how, many years ago, they decided to put on Aristophanes' *Trojan Women*. This was to be an epic production. And so it was. The whole of Singapore's cultural community seemed to be abuzz with the news that Keng Sen was readying himself for something Singaporeans had never experienced before. When it finally happened, all who had bought tickets for this show were assembled in an open car park where buses were waiting to take us to where the play was to be staged. After nearly ten miles of riding, we came to a halt. I recognized the vicinity straight away: it was an old abandoned quarry right in the middle of Singapore! Now who on earth would have ever dreamt of using this abandoned quarry (whose existence was unknown to most of the younger Singaporeans) for a theatrical production? We were puzzled, we were in doubt, we were wondering if this flamboyant director, this *enfant terrible* of the Singapore stage, knew what he was doing. Was he trying to prove something? "Yes, of course I was!" enthuses Keng Sen. "At first people were sceptical, but see what happened when they actually experienced the play. In that open space, wild with wild stories floating, wild with the haunting moonlight on certain evenings, overwhelmed with the memories of the past, people were crying openly, Kirpal. When the women's chorus incantated their lines, we saw tears flowing down on so many cheeks we started crying ourselves." And even as Keng Sen tells me this, his eyes are a little moist with memory. I remember that intense experience. For me who deals in books, for whom drama was of the essence when it came to the great fundamental conflicts of the human condition, Man versus God, yes, I remember. After watching the show as the buses brought us back to that car park where we were earlier assembled, there was absolute silence. There was no discussion, no talk, nothing, just silence. Even as we got off the buses and said our goodnights, it was clear something magical, something mysterious, had happened; we had been transformed by the touch of Keng Sen's directorial power. Even as I write this, I cannot restrain my tears!

Original. New. Different. Three words which capture well Keng Sen's creative self. Or do they, I ask Keng Sen. "Well, for me creativity is all these plus more. One has to have a vision, one has to be brave, one has to realize the heavy costs involved. Creativity is not something you just have and you just throw at others; for me it has to be internalized before it can be externalized. I usually walk around for days with ideas before I share them with anyone. Frequently I am alone not because I choose to be anti-social but because it is in this isolated state that I think best. Food, clothing, the mundane details of daily life stop to mean very much during these incubative periods. I don't quite know how to put it in cogent language, but, you know, I sort of withdraw when I feel a new idea, a new concept, brewing in my head." So when this happens and the creative grip is evident, do other things cease to be of concern? "Yes, I am afraid so," he agrees. "Some might think this is selfish on my part but I can't help it, it's the way I am. And you know I now can confidently say that this behaviour has actually been with me since young. I remember I used to lock myself in my room just thinking about a movie I might have watched or a comic strip I might have read or just an article of law I might have been writing about. Being alone and just processing — is that the word, processing? — it all has always been a large part of my creative self."

Keng Sen tells me of his present preoccupations. The Writers' Lab, which he instituted and which brings together some of the best young playwrights from around the region (and occasionally from afar), is going on extremely well. TheatreWorks is now a part of the Singaporean cultural scene with huge governmental funding and support. It is also generously supported by big commercial concerns. The company itself under Keng Sen's direction has imprinted its unique stamp on the Singaporean imagination. It has done this in big and small ways. Few can forget how TheatreWorks organized three-day long almost non-stop performances of plays designed to make people aware of their lost history, national and individual, ethnic and religious, gender-based and typecast. "When we did the Sook Ching series," says Keng Sen, "it was tough. So many different agencies, government bodies and people were involved that sometimes we thought the project would fail on account of its sheer size. But we went ahead with it, we took the risk. Instead the result was shattering! Once again we proved that with guts, courage and vision, we could win audiences and we could deliver. Again, as you know from the press write-ups and so on, people got very excited about us and what we were doing." No doubt about this. Sook Ching was a re-enactment of a very dark period in the lives of Singaporeans and Malaysians; it was about the Japanese invasion and occupation and the massacres which followed. Not a happy thing to carry on about. Keng Sen agrees. We move on.

I mention his Shakespearean productions. *Lear* and then *Desdemona*. These were big productions. Keng Sen was into his cross-cultural binge, bringing actors, musicians, dancers, technicians even, from different countries, setting them all up and making them all concentrate on producing a single play – the play of his choice. *Lear* and *Desdemona* were the two big ones. "So were you trying to do a Peter Brooks?" I ask. "You know, Kirpal," he replies. "so many people have mentioned that name to me and guess what? I have never met the man! Obviously I have read about him, seen a couple of his productions – mainly on video – but I don't know him, so when people compare me with him I am always astounded. I take it as a compliment. I mean, Brooks is big, isn't he? (I nod). Well, as you know, my Shakespearean productions, except maybe *Hamlet*, have all been controversial but I don't basically care very much. People can say whatever they want to, for me it is enough that a job got done." "But surely the adverse criticism must upset you, worry you?" I want to know. "Yes," he replies, "but I can't afford to let that bother me too much or else I won't be able to work! So I move on. I knew I was badly done by after *Desdemona*, people just didn't understand what I was doing, maybe I was too '**out there**', but I am grateful for the experience. I learnt a lot. I learnt, especially, that you can't go too far out even when you want to be creative! But I must say my actors, musicians, helpmates from so many different cultural backgrounds with such a rich storehouse of cultural memories, they all concentrated and put on terrific performances, night after night. It was exhausting, but thrilling and most rewarding. I believe in cross-cultural theatrical collaborations and engagements. I think they test us, put us through a lot of soul-searching. In the end, though, I think we have to return to cultural specifics." So I ask what he was up to then.

"Lately I have been working on something both nearer home but also further. Further because not many of us want to talk about this, know this or even remember this." I am curious. My eyes ask "What?" "Well," he goes on, "I have been thinking about three countries around us but about whom we in Singapore know precious little. Vietnam, Laos and Cambodia. Especially Laos and Cambodia. I am exploring how the religious and spiritual lives of these countries intertwine with the ordinary lives of the people. It is part of the CAP (the Continuum Asia Project) – like the Young Writers' Lab and the Flying Circus Project, this is yet another of Keng Sen's original ideas. In some ways it is a continuing journey after *The Killing Fields* (Keng Sen's production, *not* the film of the same name but obviously bearing similarities). But I want to bring in monks, government officials, military men, the ordinary people and explore what truly happened in those dark, gruesome years under Pol Pot. It is part of my documentary performance theme. Theatre for me cannot be just simple entertainment anymore. As I reach 40 years I realize life has to open its wounds and show people what reality is and was. This is risky, even dangerous work, but it must be done. I must reveal truths about horror, the horror of war, the horror of terrorism, the horror of just plain, blind dictatorship. For us in this region Pol Pot's regime brought our own sense of the Holocaust. I want to show this in Germany and see what they think, how they respond. I want to show this in Singapore, anywhere and everywhere because I believe we cannot ignore the lessons which history teaches us. But I have to soak myself in the cultural life of the Cambodians. So I am getting ready to go there."

Keng Sen has been to Cambodia and has staged his Cambodian project in Germany and Vienna. Like the many other Ong Keng Sen productions, these latest ones draw huge crowds and get him new fellowships, awards and recognition. This director has done his thing at the Lincoln Center, the Kennedy Center, in Australia, Japan, London and several other big cities in Europe. He has arrived, and he is not yet 40. As I go through the final page proofs of this book, I read with delight the news that Keng Sen has just been given Singapore's highest award for cultural distinction – The Cultural Medallion. Well, I guess this means more muscle to him, and with good reason too, for he fought hard and never flinched.

In a moving email he sent me long after this interview, he told me how he had managed to pack his father's writing desk only three years after the old man's passing. He and his mother talked about the old days. As I write this and reflect on this young man's achievements, I tell myself creativity is about having a vision, a commitment and about having the courage and passion to be true to oneself.

Anita Rodick
Creating a New Corporate Order

Space. Space. And more space. This is what I am thinking about as my friend Peter Tyson, drives me into the lovely lush grounds where the famous Anita Rodick lives. This is your true, your real English countryside, and within the spacious grounds, the size of which boggles me coming from tiny Singapore, is the mansion in which Anita lives. As she comes to greet us I notice just how radiant and **vital** she is – she speaks in a clear, if a little accentuated, voice. I am in awe of this world-famous woman. It has been my good fortune to have met some of the best minds of the 20th century, but to be in the presence of a woman who has become a household name in the field of business usually dominated by men – wow! That, I feel is an altogether separate blessing.

Because I am impressed by the sheer size of the house in which she lives, I take this as a convenient starting point: "Does space mean a lot to you?" "Yes," answers Anita, and continues, "From young I have been very conscious of space. I think it is critical for all of us, particularly the young, to have space, in every sense of that word. In my travels around the world one of the things I have found is that very few people, especially women, have enough space. It is a bad condition to be in, you know, when you don't have space!" I wonder if, true to her reputation, Anita has started on a feminist angle. "I don't know how much you know about the relationship between space and freedom, Kirpal," she adds, "but for me, space is vital if you want to be free. I remember as a young girl, one of the things I valued very highly was my private space. I was frequently left alone and to my own devices. The grown-ups were busy doing their thing and I had the good fortune of being free to do mostly what I liked. So I walked a lot, talked to myself quite a bit and read a lot. But I managed all this only because I had space. You know what I mean?"

Of course I knew what she meant! Had I not roamed the old hills of Batu Gajah in Malaysia and walked miles in abandoned tin mines, vast fields of space now again under threat of being used for building some factory or other? Do creative people need this space in order to be creative? "Well, about that I am not 100% sure," Anita tells me, "but I do know that for me space does play a big role in the way I think. The moment I could afford it, I bought a house with a large enough garden so that I can take walks and breathe the fresh air and hear the birds sing sometimes." And looking quizzically out towards the trees (seated on a bench in the garden, we are drinking tea and the sun is just about to set behind the roof of this huge house), she asks, "Did you hear any bird sing as you drove here?" "Yes," I answer, "it was the sound of a small bird." "Probably a robin," Anita says, and we get back to the more serious business of our meeting.

In connection with all of this it is important to note that Anita Rodick's house is full of treasures; from old, sentimental hand-me-downs (she is ever so proud of what her grandmother has given her) to some of the more dramatic paintings of our time (I recognize Andy Warhol's *Mao*, for example, among many other famous paintings hanging practically on every wall in the house) to the sculptures which adorn the large lawns (in one section there are some hundred sculptures all standing in a posture which can be unnerving) – everywhere there are treasures. But I do not ask her about her wealth. Rather, I ask, "Tell me about some of your youthful adventures." She replies, "Well, I didn't have too many adventures, you know. Those days girls didn't get up to much around here, but yes, I had my fair share of fun, of escapades, doing my own thing, as it were. I read a lot and my teachers seemed very pleased about this and encouraged me. I could have been a writer like you (she laughs) – I remember acting. I played **Joan of Arc**, and I used to role-play and imagined myself as being this or that. I lost my father when I was ten and I must say I didn't like that very much. I was influenced by the authors whose books I devoured: John Steinbeck, Dorothea Lang, also my grandfather made an impact on me. He was a circus owner and I remember marvelling at his circus animals and the clowns and the trapeze artists. I wanted to be a photographer; I thought I was very creative and possessed a creative eye. I was active, very, very active and I seemed to have loads of energy to do many things. My mother used to rein me in every time she thought I was going off somewhere to do my own thing! I used to make up stories, you know, of knights in shining armour, etc. Well, that was before I got to know just how greedy and selfish and horrible men can be!" I laugh. "Yes, Kirpal," she adds, "I have known some pretty bad men in my life! And if you ask me to say it I will say that **greed** is the greatest problem which men somehow don't know how to solve. There is plenty of so-called **male bonding** but in spite of everything men don't know how to handle greed!" I sense she is getting worked up, so I distract her by asking about her mother. "You know, my mother doesn't want to stay with me here; she says she is too far away from where the action is (London) so that the entire section of the house I showed you remains unused mostly. Is your mother, too, averse to staying with you?" Not expecting to be asked about my mother (whom I have not met since I was very young) I shift focus again.

"Did you begin **The Body Shop** alone?" I ask. "Well, yes and no. You can never really **begin** anything alone, certainly not on the scale of The Body Shop, but yes, it was my idea. I wanted to show that you could have good, high-quality health products, body cleansers, soaps and the like, without having to hurt, harm or maim animals. It was all, I suppose, akin to the Greenpeace movement like, I wanted to show that health is holistic and requires a holistic approach. The Body Shop was meant to be holistic in its approach. I gave every single employee the full freedom to raise questions, to put in views, to discuss his or her role within the business. I wanted every single person associated with The Body Shop, from the people who supplied the raw materials to those who manufactured our products to those who marketed and sold them, I wanted every one to be part of the process of The Body Shop. For me The Body Shop was not simply something to make money; it was a **philosophy**, it was meant to be **a way of life and living**. The Body Shop has changed a lot, a lot and I am no longer directly involved in its running anymore, but in 1976 when I got it going, well, at that time I knew exactly what I wanted to see happen and it did! I did not care for business paradigms and management rules or principles. I just wanted a happy family to run a happy business. When the business got good I started giving a lot of money to charities, to women's organizations all over the world because I had seen just how hard these women worked, whether in Tahiti or the Pacific islands, or Bangladesh or Indonesia, or Ghana or Brazil; everywhere they were exploited and I wanted to try and lessen their burden a little bit. In the early days we saw ourselves as part of an experiment, an exploration, if you like. We valued a bottom-up scheme, we didn't have any five-year plans, we didn't hire strategists. We wanted to show the world we could do it, that we could manage a business which was healthy and wholesome. Very soon The Body Shop became as much a **political** concern as a simple business venture. I wanted a company with an **attitude** and The Body Shop had an attitude. When we were younger we knew the first names of every employee and no employee had a job description. Now everything is changed. We have become a billion-dollar industry and I am not sure if we have got it right."

Anita is visibly agitated. She hands me a speech she gave on 5 May 1998 to the well-known advertising firm Ogilvy & Mather. Her talk was entitled "**How Creativity Improves the Bottom Line of Business**". As she pours more tea for both of us I quickly glance at the article and pick up a few points of great interest to me. "You said in this speech, Anita, that creativity was a 'mystery' to you.

Have you changed your opinion about this?" I ask. "No," she replies. "On the contrary, I am even more convinced now than I ever was about the essential mystery of creativity. I still see mystery everywhere as I stated in that speech. And I still believe in what I said then through the different quotes I gave: "**Imagination is more important than knowledge**" (Einstein), "**You have to systematically create confusion, it sets creativity free**" (Dali). As I said then, Kirpal, each of us carries an inward map on which are transcribed the places, events and people that are known to us and who shape our thinking. I don't know what creativity is; I'll probably go to the grave not knowing what it is!" I ask a second question arising out of this key 1998 document in my hands: "Do you still believe that things like design and communication are crucial to the success of a creative business venture?" "Absolutely," she replies. "I believe every word I said then, Kirpal. You can just quote me. I mean The Body Shop has had its fuck-ups, for instance we truly believe that **posters on windows** make a huge difference to the way people look at your shop and its products. So we had this Acid poster – now that was a total screw-up. But we learnt a lesson, had a good laugh, and moved on. You must take risks, Kirpal, real big risks if you want to make it big. You can just play it safe all the time. We never played it safe. We took risks. We still do though nowadays I have very little to do with the actual running of the company because I have sold off most of my interests in it. But I can tell you, I can say that in those glorious early days of The Body Shop, work was an extension of my kitchen, my home. We did more than just buy and sell. People fell in and out of love. Employees talked. We experimented. I learnt that **you can bring your heart to work with you**. That was important – it made a big difference to work attitude and to work ethic – and yes, you asked about communication. As I said then and will say it again now, for me **communication** is fundamental to a creative culture. As soon as I was convinced that things such as plans, charts, reports, systems and procedures were creativity deadening, I immediately started **creative conversations** where we meet once or twice every month to just share creative ideas, talk a lot and laugh a lot. You'd be surprised just how many wonderful ideas come out of such sessions, free and easy-going. Many of The Body Shop's creative successful ideas came out of such creative conversations. For example the idea of **selling your message onsite** was thrown in quite casually by one of our managers. Everything matters in right communication, from the typeface you use to the shape and design which make up your corporate identity. You must communicate right or else you fail. And in the end all of this is **not** a science, but an art. And art is fun. And there has to be fun even when you are making money. Otherwise what's the point of it all? Money for its own sake is not of much use, is it now? Travelling is important; travelling shows you things you've never seen before, maybe even never imagined before. I have learnt so much through my travels, even when I went to your beautiful little island I discovered so much about your people, the women there. So many of them asked me about what I have so often said about women's age and their beauty. Singaporean women want to grow old without wrinkles. I tell them, forget it; wrinkles are part of us and we should live with them. Beauty is more than just worrying about wrinkles." I reflect on the obsession of women everywhere – their need to be beautiful as defined by media hype. Anita continues, "The media is powerful but more powerful than even the media is the way individuals think. If you can change the way people think, Kirpal, you can change anything. And for this you need courage. Change is courage. The Body Shop has always remained open to change. For instance most people want to separate politics from business; I don't believe you ever can. At The Body Shop we turn our shops into **action stations**, places for making customers think about animal rights, human rights, etc. We use everything we can, good poetry, quotations from the great philosophers. Many of these are controversial; they therefore become conversation pieces, topics for people to talk about as they have their coffee or lunch in those big shopping malls. We do everything we can to make individuals think and make them think differently from what the popular media tells them. Business must be about the public good and not private greed."

We keep talking until it is dark. My hosts – the Tysons – have left. I see that Anita and I have been talking for more than four hours – longer than either of us had planned. I put to her one last question: "How do you see yourself?" "Oh," answers Anita, "as I always have – a rebel. I have always harboured radical thoughts.

You may have heard that nowadays I am a political activist, much more than ever before. Indeed my own activities these days are kept quite distinct from those of The Body Shop. As I said in that 1998 speech again – god, that speech was damned important! – I see myself as a gadfly, an irritant, someone who annoys you by asking awkward and hard questions. Many people don't like me, you know, Kirpal, I should warn and caution you as you put all this into your book!"

Indeed. As a farewell gesture, Anita offers to drive me to the train station. As I pack my things, she hands me two books. In one of them, *Take It Personally: How Globalization Affects You and Powerful Ways to Challenge It*, she inscribes, "This book, Kirpal – I am so proud of. Enjoy. Anita Rodick." The word "so" is underlined. I look at the contents and there are contributions by well-known personalities such as Ralph Nader, Aung San Suu Kyi, Paul Hawken, Maude Berlow and by organizations like The Ruckus Society, Global Exchange and Multinational Monitor. As I put the book away, I register the quotation on the back cover: "**What is needed now is a revolution in kindness**." More than once in my interview, Anita had referred to kindness. I tell Anita as she drives us slowly out of her beautiful garden, about my work on Aldous Huxley. Her face lights up. She says, "Good old Aldous; he, too, wanted us to be kind."

Peter Doggett
Working Across Cultures

To walk to Peter Doggett's office in the plush buildings which house the senior executives of Seaworld is to go through a maze. Along the corridors, on the walls on either side, are huge posters showing people performing at Seaworld, as well as the many countries around the world from where the visitors come flocking to this great entertainment venue in the largest island in the world. The Gold Coast itself, where Seaworld is situated, has a global reputation for having some of the finest sandy beaches around. After some walking and climbing of steps I reach the man himself! Peter is tall, big by Asian standards. He gives me a strong hug while his lovely secretary looks on. "So you found your way here, Kirpal, not a bad feat. Creative, wouldn't you say?" He is being cheeky, referring to the hideaway otherwise known as the Office of the International Marketing Director where we are now meeting for this interview. Peter has a twinkle in his eye, a twinkle about which I tease him in return: "You are not going to tell me that your charm is also creative!" We laugh. I have known Peter for many years and all through them I have watched how he has progressed and brought to Seaworld more and more people from all over the world.

We begin by my asking him a simple, straightforward question: what, in his background did he think made his outlook on life a **creative** one? He laughs; his eyes light up; he looks up at the ceiling and says, "Nothing. I don't think there was anything in my upbringing which I can confidently say made me think about creativity. I had a pretty normal childhood; the family wasn't rich or anything; Mum and Dad went about their own business; we kids were basically left to our own devices and I'll just say I grew up like all the other kids. Nothing unusual." "You sure about this, mate?" I pester him. "Yes," he replies, "mine was a boring childhood. Well, I did sing in the church choir – but that's not creative, is it?" I could see that Peter was not going to open himself to too many probing questions without effort. It is in his nature to be subtle and oblique. On top of this, Peter is one of the most modest men I have ever known; humility comes naturally to him and it has never ceased to amaze me how he has been able to retain those precious qualities of simple charm and basic human decency, given the highly competitive world in which he has triumphed for more than 20 years. "If you think, Kirpal," he continues, "that creativity is something which parents instil in their growing kids, think again. Well, it doesn't happen here, it didn't happen in my family and I doubt very much if it happens in many other Australian families. We don't think about creativity in a conscious kind of way. Well, at least not until some foreign bloke wearing a turban comes along and starts prodding and probing!" I persist, "You're a charmer, Peter, but surely it has not been just charm which has made Seaworld what it is today, even from the first time I came here about 17 years ago!"

"I think," Peter says calmly, staring straight at the office wall, "there were two or three individuals who showed me how to be different, how to survive in tough times and how to get around awkward problems. Much of what I do today can be stated in these terms: how to be different and survive in tough times." I look at him and I see a man for whom life has not always been easy. A man who has had to put in his fair share of struggle in order to climb the corporate ladder. "I spent some time dabbling in politics and there I learnt a lot. To succeed in politics takes guts, just as it takes guts to be creative. Not all of us have this quality – guts. I remember how I managed a small political coup by correctly drafting a letter which stirred up so many passions it gave me my first taste of success! Looking back I'd say that experience of knowing that just by using the right words one could achieve so much left a lasting impression on me. I realized the power of words, of language and I have always remembered that! In school I used to love debating and that, too, made me conscious of how to use the right words, the right language for the right purposes."

This is interesting to me, for I have a firm belief in the power of words and language to fuel the creative imagination. So I push him a little further. "Suppose, Peter," I say, "you were drafting an advertisement for Seaworld now, would you still concentrate on the words? Or would you let the visuals do the work?" He sits up and thinks for a while; Peter is not the type to answer you immediately. "Yes," he says, "definitely, because even though they say a picture tells a thousand words, you get one word wrong and that's it – the damage is done! You can't recover the losses. Whenever I talk with people around the world I look at their faces; I watch their eye movements; I observe the way their bodies shift and move; I notice how they speak to me, whether directly or indirectly by looking at someone else in the room – because people get very affected by the words they say and the words you say to them. I was once with this Japanese guy and I wanted him to help me bring thousands of Japanese tourists here, that's my job. So we met, drank *sake* – and it is vital that you drink *sake* if you want Japanese business – and ate. He hardly said much, partly because he was hesitant about his English but more significantly because he did not want me to misunderstand anything he was going to tell me. In return I spoke slowly, too, measuring every word carefully and making sure I did not say more than I needed to or lead him to think I was either condescending or greedy for his help."

I know that for Peter communication is of the essence. So many times when we have interacted I have noticed clearly his emphasis on certain key terms in his vocabulary. I tease him about one such word now. "Peter, I know that for you being creative means knowing what the other person or people around you want, knowing how they will respond but tell me, you always talk about the **future**, is this important for creativity?" "Of course," says Peter, a big smile forming on his manly lips, "of course. I think it is crucial to anticipate the future, to be able to use your resources to extrapolate and almost predict what people are wanting to spend their money on. This is my business; this is what I have to think about all the time. It is no use being creative; even **super** creative (it is obvious that Peter is stressing this for my benefit!) if you are not able to anticipate the future. In my line of work, we need to know just how many visitors we can expect two weeks from now, three months from now, two years from now, even five years from now. We prepare projections; we produce statistics, charts and graphs, plotting demographic shifts and population relocations. For example, until recently we didn't really go out to woo New Zealand tourists to Seaworld; we just assumed they knew where we were and they'd come. But recently we have started to be more proactive there. Now, for many years we thought that the best way to get, say the Taiwanese, to come here, the Koreans, the Malaysians, even the Singaporeans, was to visit these countries twice, thrice a year, show them glossy brochures and wine and dine the key players. This worked for a while but not now. Now the tourist industry has grown more sophisticated; it needs more information and ready access to qualified experts who can discuss and share informed views, basically people on-the-spot. This is why some years ago I started to look out for local individuals who could help us promote Seaworld in their own countries. Because we got there early, we got the numbers."

Yes. I knew this was correct because Peter on his several trips to Singapore had mentioned many times the pleasure he had enjoyed when he had recruited somebody talented for the job of promoting Seaworld as a tourist destination in his or her home country. Indeed, much of Peter's success could be attributed to his good eye for getting the right people to do the right job. But I am keen to know more about his views on creativity. "But, Peter," I say, "tell me more about your own take on this whole business about creativity and innovation – is Seaworld concerned with this? Are you guys into Innovation?" "I don't spend too much time worrying about these issues, mate," says Peter. "There are people here whose job it is to create and innovate. I understand what you mean and where you are coming from. But our commercial culture is different from your intellectual culture at universities. So one thing I am personally doing – and you'll like this, I know – is to slowly find my way into these august university departments and tell them about how it is like in this real world! For me being innovative is going out there, working your butt off and trying to make people see that there could be a good synergy between, say, a university's School of Business/Marketing/Management, whatever, and our Seaworld. For me to be creative is to be adventurous, to go out and try things out. This is what I do. Even at home I tell the girls (Peter has two lovely daughters) to go out and try different things. Don't be happy just with what you have and know. You must allow your mind to be open to new ideas. That, for me, is also being innovative. You know some years ago they asked me to sit on the board of the ATC (Australian Tourist Commission) and I realized just how much work there was to get done if we were to make our country more attractive to outsiders. We Australians have always tended to be insular and quite comfortable just doing our own thing. But the world is pushing outwards now; we need to promote our goods and services worldwide. Everyone gets involved, from the airlines to the performers doing their tricks here at Seaworld. But most of these people don't know a thing about what truly goes on. This is why I wrote that handbook on doing trade in Australia. This was the first time anyone had written such a book. I thought that was creative!" Peter bursts out in a guffaw. I share it with him! After all, we had always talked a lot about cross-cultural exchanges and knowledge.

"I think in my work, being creative means also to recognize and know what people from other countries like and don't like. For instance, we take little souvenirs, gifts to give out on our various trade missions. People are sensitive about what they receive, about what you give them and how you give them. Even a small thing as *when* you give the souvenir or gift item, yes, even this matters a lot and could make a big difference whether or not you secure that contract for 5,000 people to come to Seaworld. I suppose I have been very lucky. You know those two to three persons I told you about just now? They also taught me to value the uniqueness of each person. So for me being creative is also to be able to **sense** what the people we are dealing with are about, what they appreciate, what they dislike. Too many boo-boos are made in international business and we Australians especially tend to be rather laid back about these important cultural nuances and sensitivities. Very simply, take a business name card – how do you read it? I found out that even reading a business name card requires expertise beyond just knowing how to read the printed words! So for me being creative is to know how to read the hidden text, catch the meaning of subtle gestures and appreciate the moments of revelation when dealing across cultural boundaries. As I told you yesterday, right now we have a senior member of the Saudi royal family visiting us – not everybody knows how to handle this. Does your creative or innovative genius help here? Not necessarily, not if being creative is just throwing your weight around and saying 'I am creative, I am innovative'. No. We have to find creative ways of making the members of his entourage happy and comfortable so that they will spend loads of money here and at the same time go home and tell others to visit us."

Peter, I note, is a kind of self-made man. He is a fighter. Though not brash, not one to go out and pick fights, he seldom gives in to defeat, despair or gloom. Whether it was something as small as the question of an enclosure for the dolphins or a big issue of bringing celebrities in to add lustre and glitz to Seaworld, Peter is out there sharing his opinion, giving his views. During the good years Peter succeeded in bringing in close to over 100,000 visitors from Asia to Seaworld, a feat worthy of note in itself. Of late the world economies have not been doing so fabulously and everything has slowed, but here was Peter, outlining new strategies. "I think the way forward is to go for a different kind of **niche** market, one which will bring in good money but not in terms of large numbers but small numbers who want large returns for their dollars." I ask Peter to elaborate. "Well, why don't you join us, Kirpal?" He says "Maybe you could provide some useful creative input for me to give you details without giving you secrets!"

Again, that twinkle, this time accompanied with loud laughter. Peter has arranged for me to go with him on a cruise where, he assures me, I will definitely meet many creative individuals who might share their innovative ways of surviving with me. As I get ready for this wonderful adventure I cannot help but make one last comment to him: "Peter, as always, you're a bugger but, hey, you've got a permanent fan in me, mate! Creativity does mean knowing when not to."

BRIEF NARRATIVES

I could have interviewed many, many others – the world is full of wonderfully gifted people, people whose entire lives spell "creativity". Obviously, I did not. I cannot. Here are three shorter, briefer narratives – different and differently told. These, too, illuminate and expand our understanding of creativity and creative selves...

Peter Nazareth

One fine day early in 1992 most of us at the university were surprised to see Singapore's main English newspaper, *The Straits Times*, carry a headline which read something like **Elvis Presley to feature in university course**. Naturally this aroused our curiosity and we immediately turned to the relevant pages to read what this was all about. And there, lo and behold, was the news that a professor at the University of Iowa had successfully persuaded the authorities that the life and work of the great King of Rock and Roll, Elvis Presley, was worthy of a university course! Imagine what some of the conservatives would have said. Frankly, in Singapore, most of my colleagues at the National University of Singapore were either envious or quite openly contemptuous. Those who were envious wanted similarly exciting courses to be available at our university; those who were contemptuous thought the whole idea silly and beneath academic respectability. For the latter group, **what next**? As if this course on Elvis was going to ruin completely their own pretensions to scholarly work!

I had first been introduced to the man behind the Elvis proposal by a graduate student and writer from Uganda called Theo Luzuka. Theo had come to Singapore in the late 70s to work on Indian literature and we struck up a good friendship. Professor Peter Nazareth had been at Makarere College in Uganda where Theo had studied. In Uganda Peter had made a name for himself by writing a novel *The General Is Up* based mainly on the terrible reign of Idi

Amin. But by the time Theo had talked to me about Peter, Peter had already migrated to the US and was working at the University of Iowa. Of course Peter and I had become very good friends through Theo, and ironically I have since seen much much more of Peter and his family than I have of poor Theo whose own fortunes have been greatly affected by the fortunes of that sad and tragic continent Africa.

So this Peter Nazareth had now drawn world media to tiny Iowa City where a revolution had taken place! A revolution in academic terms. And what a great moment it was, for universities have been known to be completely old-fashioned, backward, always removed from the experiences of everyday life, lost in the subterfuges of their many self-created ivory towers, etc. But here was a man who had managed to put a popular icon on the university curriculum and made this feat world-famous. Anyone visiting Peter Nazareth's website will immediately recognize what a fascinating course Peter has introduced. I have, over these past six years, spent many wonderful hours and days with Peter. Apart from being a legendary host to hundreds of writers, musicians, artists and scholars who swamp him from all over the globe, Peter is an unassuming, gentle human being, always obliging and ever ready to engage in intellectual, cultural issues. His knowledge of Elvis is beyond belief! Even his house can be called a second Elvisville! So much of Elvis is present.

Peter tells me with great pride that the course, now more than a decade old, is going very strong and each year gets better as more and more students enrol. His own interests keep growing (instead of waning) and the Elvis mark is set to stay at the University of Iowa. "Who will take over from you when you retire, Peter?" I ask him. "Well," he answers, "hopefully one of my younger colleagues or someone new they might hire. It is too valuable, too good, too important, too popular a course to be dropped." And I believe him. In his other important academic life Peter is an internationally known critic, especially of post-colonial literature. He brought into academic discussion the notion of the **trickster**, the character or emblem who doubles up and both deceives as well as provides key knowledge. This concept is an intricately complex one and Peter's dexterity is plainly obvious when reading his book *The Trickster Tradition*. Here is a clear and specific example of creativity at work in a university context, a context which many of us painfully know to be frequently stuffy and stolid, with our superiors clinging to nothing more than so-called cherished old traditions of scholarly virtue. I am reminded, as a former student of literature, of the kinds of battles the hero of many of these scholarly types in literary circles, F.R. Leavis, had to fight. This is a much-maligned name these days (indeed for nearly the past three decades,) but in his time, good old Leavis was fighting his numerous battles with books which bore titles such *as New Bearings in English Poetry* and with his journal *Scrutiny*. At Cambridge they admired the man for his scholarship, but this wonderful critic was never made a full professor and remained a reader right to the very end. Such, we may say, are the pains of academia.

Sarah and the Alfred Deakin High School

All my daughters live and study in Australia. My eldest, now at the University of New South Wales where she is confronting energetically the challenges and fascinations of intellectual rigour, told me a story about how her high school in Canberra – the Alfred Deakin High School – came up with a very interesting and creative idea to raise funds. "You know how it's like, Dad," she told me, "even in Singapore we used to raise funds by organizing activities and events. Well, we decided to be different at Deakin because we wanted to raise money for a certain school project. We decided to invite the larger community (parents/friends/students from other schools) to play CowPat Bingo." "What's that ?" I asked. She explained, "CowPat Bingo. We drew sort of large squares in the school field, sold CowPat cards, got a mother-cow and her calf (borrowed for the day from a farmer outside Canberra) to grace the occasion and people got Xs (crosses) every time the calf or the mother pooed! It was so much fun, Dad, and everybody had a great time and we made quite a few bucks!" "It must have been a little, ahem, *shitty*, too," I said. "Yes," said Sarah, "but what the heck, it was a good idea and everyone, Dad, everyone had fun and a very good time." Yes, I said to myself, yes, but would many educational institutions be open to such creative ideas?

Learning from my three daughters, Sarah, Areta and Misha, has been among the most valuable of my experiences. They are all young, discovering and exploring the world around them. They fumble and fall, but in the many new things they embark on and the new experiments they try out, they learn and it is in the learning that their real education lies. I am very blessed for each is supremely creative in her own way and I can only pray that God will bless them and give them the strength and the fortitude to go forth without fear as life unfolds its own mysteries to them. This is not the place to detail the many creative things Sarah, Areta and Misha have done – all young people are creative – but merely to record a sense of joy, a sense of gratitude to all those who help these young girls realize their creative efforts. I just wish more educational institutions were open and flexible, where young learners can learn much by doing rather than just absorbing. I am not the first to state this (and neither shall I be the last) but it needs to be said, again and again, that any teacher who tries to mould his or her charges without respect for their intelligence and creative abilities is doing more harm than good. Yes, we will get the As in the examinations, we will get good, law-abiding citizens, but we will not help these young men and women fulfil their own dreams because we would have killed the very flames which kept their dreams aglow. My appeal to my colleagues in the teaching arena is, at **every** level to give our students just that much leeway for them to try out their own ideas. Hard – yes, because they can be a nuisance, but in the long-run this will pay dividends (if I have to use a material metaphor). Recall, would the beautiful mystery of our genes have been unlocked if Watson and Crick had not fouled up some equipment in those famous Cambridge labs?

Ted Skewes and the Pendleton Farm Retreat

In 1976 I found myself in Adelaide, South Australia. I was a Colombo Plan Scholar at the University of Adelaide, one of the oldest universities in the Commonwealth. One of the good things about being a Colombo Plan Scholar was that one got to know a few hosts – families and people who were there to "look after us", provide a kind of "home-away-from-home". I was very fortunate; I asked for – and got – a host from the country rather than from the city.

I still remember vividly that cold, wintry morning in April 1976 when Ted Skewes came to pick me up from the bus station at Tumby Bay on the Eyre Peninsula, some 350 miles away from Adelaide. The bus ride had been okay but my heart had been pounding with excitement. When I got down from the bus and saw this man in a typical Australian hat I knew I had met my *ocker-mate*! Over the years we have had such fun recalling that first meeting. Very few Sikhs had ever been that way and my being there was in itself a cause of much public chatter. Ted's family was huge, more like an extended Asian family than the nuclear families of the typical Western world I was familiar with. In the countryside, Ted told me, people still stayed together and cherished family values and togetherness. He managed a big farm, growing wheat (both dry and wet), barley, corn and many other types of grains which he exported as well as sold to the domestic market. There were sheep, cows, dogs, pigs, chickens (chooks!), kangaroos (my first hunting of kangaroos took place then) and foxes, on and around the farm. And all kinds of birds from the terrible galahs (which Ted hated) to the beautifully crested red-necked parrots. My stay on the farm (and all my subsequent stays with this fascinating man for I have stayed with him literally every year since!) was totally educational.

Ted had trained to be an engineer; indeed he had worked for the Highways Department in Adelaide, but the call of the land, as he put it, made him search for a bride from those parts. And he did. Sue, his wife, is one of the most warm-hearted persons I have ever met and within my family Auntie Sue has a very special place. Each time I visited Ted, he would tell me of some new idea he had, some new plan to improve the stock, some new seed to make the wheat better. I knew Ted would not stay in one place – his was a restless, creative spirit which wanted, needed and demanded, room for experimentation, space for expansion. Ted's creative side showed up frequently, whether in discussing a book ("So you think this Patrick White fella is good, huh? Listen, mate, he needs more experience in the land if he wants to talk about trees!" I had introduced Ted and Sue to Patrick White's *The Tree of Man*, about the relationship between people and nature) or in developing an idea for making money ("Tell you what, mate, plenty of money to be made just exporting pig-livers to your part of the world!") or in taking part in whatever came his way (Ted has played small roles in some big movies, the most famous being in Gallipoli).

About 15 years ago he had the break he had always yearned for. The Wesley Mission appointed him manager of their property known as Desert Park, situated about 120 miles southeast of Adelaide, in the beautiful landscape of the Keith Valley. Here Ted was totally on his own. His two daughters were now grown and Sue and he could now concentrate on turning the property into a really wonderful farm retreat. First the name was changed to Pendleton Farm Retreat. People had lost touch with real country living, Ted told me, and his aim was to develop a successful farmstay experience which would appeal to people both from within Australia as well as visitors from abroad. He wanted to show that even in a small, fairly remote part of this huge island-continent you could make a go of tourism. So he created his marketing line, "**Your Country Connection**". Pendleton was to become a "unique tourist destination of distinction". Over the years Ted has won consecutive tourism Gold Awards and given the surroundings a real feel of being new. Today Pendleton boasts of hospitality services which very few can compete with. Ted has a workforce of well-trained individuals who treat every visitor as part of the Pendleton family and I know many enjoy being at Pendleton so much that they keep coming back. Ted opened Pendleton to schools and colleges so that students can learn in an open environment. He marketed the idea to schools in Singapore, Hong Kong and Japan, and from these countries he gets visitors and tour groups every year.

I asked Ted what he truly thought made it all so wonderful and he said, "Mate, in one word it would be **vision**. I have always had a vision of what I want to do and achieve. I work at it. God has blessed me with some creativity which I link to my vision, and with the help of my good wife Sue and friends like you I work to realize this vision. It will surprise you (laughing) if I told you just how many hours I spend driving around Pendleton, just driving or even walking, and thinking **how I can make all this better**. I now have a new vision, one which I am sharing with my bosses. Hopefully it will be taken on board. I am working on it!"

I think back over the 27 years I have known Ted – never one to give up, always striving for the better. He has been hurt a few times, once or twice very badly, but he has always persevered and carried on. Now at 56 years he still works as hard as I have ever known him. Not one to sit on his laurels, Ted has demonstrated to me just how important it is never to say, "**I give up**". And to keep the fires of dreams and visions burning.

"**Without a vision my people shall perish**." Was Isaiah talking about only **his** people? I always tell my Christian friends, there is so much creativity in the Bible and so much creativity in the life and work of Jesus Christ. If only, if only, the followers today who spout the Scripture would be honest and true to the spirit for "**the letter killeth even as the spirit giveth abundant life**".

CONCLUSIONS

Was it Einstein who said that the difference between stupidity and genius is that genius knows its limits?

Well, I will not, dear reader, tease you again and give you many different versions of a **conclusion**. But ending this book is going to be tough, for how does one end a book which is trying to explore a concept, a happening, a frame of reference, which can, perhaps, never be fully understood, grasped, defined or explained?

To be creative is to be different, but is being different being creative? I guess the answer will have to be **no** followed by, well, it will depend a lot on the context.

My good friend David Ho, managing director of Windmill International, sent me the following email when I asked him what his take on creativity was:

> This is the key question in today's education environment ... I have attended a feedback session with NUS (National University of Singapore) on this...
>
> My humble view is that creativity is not everything to everybody ... and a password for success in ordinary life. Definitely if you don't have creativity, I don't think you can innovate. However, innovation is not creativity. Let's handle the simple part first. You innovate because there is a problem and you get around it. That is innovation. For example, if you need to go from point A to point B at the shortest possible time, you invent whatever you can to get there in quick time ... from a bicycle to motorcycle to a car.
>
> Creativity, on the other hand, demands that we think and act in different ways from the norm. We start with small things – some mischief, some nuisance, some fun, some nonsense, then we go about being creative at a national level, then at an international level. However, if we don't allow our students to create a bit of nonsense to challenge their own creativity, then nothing can be achieved from the very beginning – how can we channel constructive creativity? I think this is what the government wants

and (it) is hardly possible. You cannot tell the students to be only creative in good things; you must allow for some bad, some good, and some nonsense, but be creative nonetheless. For example, it will take a lot of creativity to raid Eusoff College (in our time this used to be the women's hostel and we boys used to go on **raids**) at night and not be caught!

Yes, we can within a generation build a creative culture in Singapore – the liberalization of art forms, music, sports, political freedom, free speech and personal expressions – and encourage our students to speak up, and the teachers to accept that when a student speaks up, they should not be offended; we need to change ground rules.

We need to change ground rules. Well worth repeating that. There are, of course, too many loose-ends which beg the issue – I mean people have been wanting to change ground rules since Day One. But the point to note, really, is that David's response encapsulates quite a few key questions this book has been dealing with and I am glad he has addressed them directly and bluntly. My generation was brought up on the survival game; we did everything we could to survive and this often meant bending rules (whether set by parents, teachers or the law itself!), finding short cuts (which frequently landed us into deep and troubled waters!) and creating new reference points if we had to. Singapore's ambassador to the United Nations, Mr Kishore Mahbubani (who wrote that provocative and insightful book, *Can Asians Think?*) was my senior at the university and I remember he was always telling us stories, jokes and anecdotes which all pointed to one main direction: originality. Kishore always wanted to do things differently; he always had a different point of view, an original point of view. In his clear, critically analytical mind (I remember him to be one of the very few in my time who obtained a First Class Honours – in Philosophy to boot!) Kishore wrote articles for the student newspaper, *The Undergrad* which sometimes got him into difficulties with the authorities. But did he give up? Or run away? No, he stood his ground, did what needed doing and moved on. My generation was thankful it had such individuals to serve as living examples to the cause of creativity – in thought and deed.

Sometimes. Yes. Sometimes. Sometimes we are all very creative and oftentimes not. My friend Naffi says his ideas run before him (well, I tell him, better that than if they ran after him!) When I discussed with him my contentious statements about creativity's link to language, he said, "One good way of discussing this is by looking at Fortune's Top 500 and seeing how many come from non-English speaking countries." I agree. But the actual checking of this is not the essence of my contention – what is, is the way, the manner in which a language handles the scope and context for creativity. Good research needs to be done in this crucial area.

Many have made their way to the top in corporate businesses by sheer hard work. Most of the rags-to-riches stories are interesting but not always for their contribution to creative thinking. Many of our forefathers belong to this category: they worked their guts out and accumulated whatever wealth they could. Some built business empires. But like the biblical statement points out, and which many can't fully grasp, "Many are called but few are chosen." So many empires are built; few last. Entrepreneurs depend on creative ideas to help them make, usually, their first dollar; alas, too many forget too soon the role of creativity in their organizations and they build solid structures which truly impress but often lie deserted when times get bad. Like in *Ozymandias*, that famous sonnet by Shelley which humbles all who read it, these empires, tall and imposing, caution us to **look and despair**. Hard work is very, very good and has to be encouraged and rewarded, but in itself it is not equal to creativity.

In Malaysia one of the all-time great narratives of creative ideas making megabucks is the story of that humble man, Lim Goh Tong. At the age of 50, when most men rest and take pride in their achievements, Lim was busy thinking about how to transform an enormous plot of jungle land on the top of a mountain into a casino and theme park in a country which was struggling to enter the New Economy. Lim had little education and little money but a big mind and a strong heart. He obtained permission for his pursuits, laid meticulous plans and garnered enough support for his dream project to become a reality. Today Genting Corporation probably has an asset base exceeding several billions. Lim's case is one of many which point to the interesting contrast between possessing education (formal education, degrees and qualifications) and creativity.

India's great prime minister, Jawaharlal Nehru, once said, "If creative imagination is lacking, our growth becomes more and more stunted, which is a sign of decay." I say here that we are today going through one of the most challenging periods we have ever faced, and we need strong-minded creative people to help us get through these tough times. Though George Bernard Shaw was known best for his wit, his witty remarks are good for more than just a laugh. Listen to what he said about people who are creative, the different ones: "All reasonable men adapt themselves to the world. Only a few unreasonable ones persist in trying to adapt the world to them. All progress in the world depends on these unreasonable men and their innovative and often non-conformist actions."

For too long we have tended to be nothing more than **reasonable**; our schools, universities, homes have all tended to turn us into reasonable people doing reasonable things in a reasonable way. Yes, this process makes us safe and stable. And also complacent, smug, soft and weak. Those of us who have read *The Time Machine*, H.G. Wells' frightening account of the future, know that reasonable people end up like the Eloi with the real creative energies belonging to the Morlocks. When I was young and saw a film version of this tragically moving tale, I was horrified at what was done to the Eloi – they had been portrayed so beautifully as being supremely happy people. Now I know better – layers of irony lie embedded in this powerful book – and a book, by the way, which most of the self-appointed literary pundits will decry as being not well-written. I now begin to appreciate more carefully what many of the great minds of humankind, from Socrates to Einstein, have stated again and again: we must not confuse, or mix up our schooling with our education. Sadly, in most countries, it is schooling which gets prioritized, not education.

I asked one of Singapore's top visual artists, Chandrasekaran, whether he thought creativity can be taught. This is what he said: "Creativity can't be read from books, it needs a holistic approach, from drinking a cup of coffee to finishing a thesis. It has to come from the mind to the mouth and from the soul to hand." Chandra is committed to his aesthetics and every one of his paintings tells a story just as every installation he has ever done has been the focus of an intense inner-search for that totality he describes. We need to listen with our own inner ears to such wonderfully creative people like the Chandra's of the world to help us understand creativity better.

So frequently have people tended to associate creativity with just the arts that it is important for all of us to know and to note and spread the word that creativity is more than just the arts: it concerns us in all areas of living. Our total human experience will be very different if we applied more creativity to all the big and small things we do every single day. I tell my Creative Thinking students at the university and all the participants of my creativity/ innovation workshops, "Lie back, close your eyes and think of the last time you were creative. Give yourself a gift for being creative that time. Now think how you are going to be creative tomorrow." They write to me and tell me what a difference this simple exercise makes to their attitude, to their thinking. So when so many ask me if creativity can be taught, I am often nowadays tempted to say, yes. Big time.

One of Malaysia's best-known literary talents, who has lived and worked in the US for almost 40 years, writer and now professor of English at the University of California at Santa Barbara, Shirley Geok-Lin Lim, has this to say:

> Creativity is not synonymous with genius or talent, for which there are innate forces – neural wirings, physical and psychical structures – that result in superior achievement. Certain societies and times have been more sympathetic to the nurturing of creativity. Most consider creativity to be an attribute, but I define creativity as a set of individual, social and cultural confluences. Individual curiosity, courage, coupled with intelligence and persistence; more, institutional systems (challenging educational, arts, science and technology centres), social and community rewards. Creative individuals breed more creative individuals. A high bar for excellence, a low threshold for repressive top-down authority. Creativity cannot be ordered; it makes its own order.

When I pushed her to tell me what made her creative, here came the reply:

> I think over-reading – long hours a day – together with physical restlessness – over-abundant energy – are my explanations for my early creativity; both resulted in curiosity, a certain extreme

individual construction of experience. I think of William Blake when I think of creativity.

William Blake – that name again. By now my readers will know my predilection for this strange genius, strangely misunderstood by so many. But, to further Shirley's point, creative people do spend many long hours alone, often just reading, and they do possess a very deep sense of curiosity. Of course creative people occasionally go mad; well, we all do; indeed it was the more **rational** people who went mad in Europe's ironically named Age of Enlightenment. I recall reading that curious couplet which the great Pope wrote when he was, I am told, only 14:

> I am His Highness' dog at Kew
> Pray tell me Sir, whose dog are you?

Well, Pope's great gift for writing satirical verse is obvious even from this one couplet – it has bite, and boy, does it bite, especially those who belong to the category of being someone's **dog** ... I think most of us do, we have been there! My cousin Charan used to have a text on the back of his entrance door (in my part of the world most guests take off their shoes when they enter a house; when they are leaving they have to put their shoes on again and because most times the shoes are neatly stowed away at the back of the main entrance door, most get to read this text as they put on their shoes):

> All guests give pleasure, some by coming, and others by going.

Well, Charan tells me, many stay back for that one-for-the-road drink which my cousin tells them to have before leaving!

In March 2002 I had the privilege of being invited to talk at the 13th Annual Meeting of the AMI (Association for Managers of Innovation). It was held in the posh Hyatt Hotel in San Diego, California. Apart from enjoying the beautiful city and its beautiful people, I learnt so much from this exciting group of people, each in his and her own way, uniquely creative and bringing new visions, new ideas to bear. I want to share just what one of them said to me about creativity. Mike Cafasso of the Pueblo Bank & Trust said,

> Creativity is ... the ability to see from a unique or original perspective ... a way of blending thoughts and perceptions about a particular vision, action, idea to enable a move towards

innovation with the hopeful result being the creation of a product, solution or another new idea.

Let's hang on to that special word, "see". In ancient times there was a category of gifted people known as **seers**. Like the famed Tiresius, these seers saw more, much much more than any one around them and sometimes they shared what they saw with others; often to their own detriment because authorities didn't always like what they heard! But, yes, to **see** new possibilities, fuse various branches of knowledge to come up with something brand new – this is certainly one important dimension of being creative. Adaptation in itself is not necessarily creative, but when the adaptation becomes so far removed from the original, then, I think, adaptation becomes creativity. Returning to the example of Japan – and this will clearly suggest where *I* draw the line between creativity and innovation – well, Japan adapted many, many of the products it imported from elsewhere. Sometimes it adapted so well that we can say it **innovated**. But, chiefly, it did not create. I recall the story of the Scotsman who wanted to prove that he could make some money by selling a jigsaw puzzle which people had no given picture to work from. Wow! Now I thought **that** was creative – if he had only designed a new kind of packaging for jigsaw puzzles, or increased their number (to 100,000 pieces, say) or even made jigsaw puzzles interactive, I'd have said he had only **innovated**. But, man, when he announced that anyone who could put those 5,000 pieces together with zero guidance could take away a million pounds, wow, that must be said to be creative but I have to confess that the words **creativity** and **innovation** are frequently used interchangeably. I was recently asked to give a talk at an event organized by Singapore's Ministry of Education. The theme for this event was Creativity and Innovation. My speech entitled, Embracing Change and Breaking Free, was delivered to an audience consisting mainly of educationists (principals, subject heads, teachers) and again, this issue arose – what is the difference between creativity and innovation? I responded by saying that though difficult, one way I distinguish between the two is to say creativity comes **before** innovation, so innovation could be said to be **applied** creativity. Creativity, for me, dwells chiefly and importantly in the realm of ideas whereas innovation manifests itself in the practical worlds of everyday realities. Thus when Leonardo da Vinci made drawings of flying birds (precursors of the modern aeroplane), he was being creative. But it took nearly 300 years for this creativity to turn into innovation. The time-lag for creative ideas to become practical innovations depends very much on contexts and community cultures. Sometimes (as, say, in the fields of music, poetry, dance, art) these conversions come fast; other times (as, say, in the fields of medicine, engineering, architecture) they come more slowly. Whether or not a creative idea becomes an innovative fact does not have very much to do with the quality or genius of the idea itself (even if many are persuaded to think so!); rather it merely suggests that at a given time and place, the decision is to turn a certain creative idea into a definite practical fact. Of course, the speed of technological change complicates the equation even more since nowadays we are experiencing rapid technological shifts which promise huge conversions of creativity into innovation.

Of course some of you, dear readers, will not agree. And naturally so. We all have our individual takes on this fascinatingly knotty subject. My good friend Dennis Haskell, a noted poet and scholar from the Antipodes, says,

> I don't really know or remember how I came to write poetry. I came from a background which was working class and entirely non-literary; we didn't have books in the house, etc. However, I realized after I left school that I had actually liked some of the English lessons and I did start reading literature. It was at university where I started writing, but I knew no one else who was interested. I started writing short stories. I did some night courses run by the Workers Educational Association, one run by a novelist and one by a theatre person on playwriting. So poetry was the third genre I tried, not the first. I think I was influenced by the popular music of the time – I was very interested in folk music, and used to go to folk clubs; and, of course, Simon & Garfunkel, Bob Dylan, Joni Mitchell and others were in their heyday.

I think the kind of education needed to make people creative is in some ways the opposite of the education they get through school and university. I used to tell the Creative Writing students at the beginning of their course that we would try to get them to unlearn the way they had been taught to think. The whole education system, not just in the west, is oriented towards reasoning and science, so that students are taught to handle abstract, conceptual thinking. We want them to have a sense of concrete experience to go with that. Picasso said that he spent his whole adult life trying to see with the eye of a child, and that makes sense to me. Students do need a lot of freedom and encouragement; in the end you can't teach creativity; you can only encourage it. Some of that comes from seeing what others have done with their creativity, some with exercises to develop perceptiveness and sensory awareness.

Well, we are back to background, cultural dimensions and education. Especially education. We cannot underestimate the significance of education in the nurturing and fostering of creativity. And yet most educational pedagogues disregard this every time they insist on examinations and testing. We in Singapore are among the world's most exam-obsessed nations and we are not too high on the creativity scales. Education must go through a reformation, we must develop in our students, particularly when they are young and fresh, this insatiable urge/desire/need to be curious and creative. We cannot be over-anxious about them passing exams and tests; we need to give them much-needed space and room to breathe. I recall many a time my teachers used to comment in my report card, "Still room for improvement" and by this they always meant I could have done better in my examinations. I don't think they meant room for my creative urges!

There is this story of a man who was seen carrying two babies in his arms. A woman walks up to him and says, "They're adorable! Which is the boy and which is the girl?" The man keeps quiet. The woman asks again, "Which is the boy and which is the girl?" The man, visibly annoyed, replied, "I don't know." Equally frustrated at not getting her answer, the woman scolds, "What kind of a father are you? You don't even know the sex of your babies!" "I'm sorry, madam," replied the irritated man, "these are NOT my babies. They're complaints arising from some condom problems. I'm just a condom salesman."

Well, God bless my teachers. Over the years, I have met and re-met many of them and I remember many who have passed on. My best teachers were those who laughed with me, showed me different ways of doing things and always said things like "If you are given a lemon, Kirpal, make lemonade" or "Never be afraid of what you do – hold your head high and people will always respect you for that". Many of my generation ruefully reflect and wonder if teachers these days show this same personal regard for pupils in their charge. I hope they do, for to have good, caring and nurturing teachers is one of life's great blessings. And it certainly augurs well for creativity! For without that gentle push, creativity can sometimes remain latent and never manifest itself.

CODA

Even as I type these words, my students here at the university are busy with their new debating championship involving more than 100 other students from the universities, polytechnics and junior colleges. They've called the championship – The Hammer Championship. So I ask one of them whether he knows of a similar name anywhere else in the world. "No, Prof, I don't think so. We have checked many websites and none carries this name." Good, I said to him. Congratulations. I believe when we come across something, some event, occurrence, game or activity which strikes us as being new, different, original, creative, we should congratulate those behind it. Because creative people do need and require (and indeed desire!) recognition. They are human, very human, and their recognition leads them to be yet even more creative.

Singapore's main news daily, *The Straits Times*, carried in its 8 May edition, an interview with the country's ambassador to the US, Professor Chan Heng Chee, an ex-colleague of mine when we both taught at the University of Singapore. When asked the question, **"What could Singapore learn from the US?"** the ambassador replied, **"Creativity**." Prof Chan points out that she will miss the creative environment which the US so blatantly provides. The level of intellectual debate and discussion (presumably as provided by the media and people) is much higher and, says, Prof Chan, Singaporeans can learn much from the way in which the US conducts itself. I agree. I have, especially in the past five years, observed the manner in which this rich, big nation has managed to steer itself to great heights in almost every sphere of life, from the pure research arena to the applied military arena. There has to be some quality, some aspect of the country's total culture which stimulates and encourages its citizens to be bold, creative and innovative. Yes, we can all learn a lot from it.

From little things to big ones, from small spaces to large ones, from the local to the global, there are umpteen opportunities for those who are creative. But there has to be nurturing, good, robust, nurturing so that the creative spark is kept alive, burning brightly. In the recent 13th Annual Conference of the ACA (American Creativity Association) held in Philadelphia, I was struck by the many diverse events and activities (with the well-known Robert Alan Black, author of *Broken Crayons: Break the Crayons and Draw Outside the Lines*, offering all delegates a galore of little thingies to keep us stimulated, engaged and creative!) which were on offer to balance the more traditional offering of serious Papers and Addresses. I believe in these methods. I have always tried to make some difference wherever I have been given an opportunity to do so. Alas, many around me are usually afraid, always wondering whether our bosses, the people **in-charge** will be offended, etc. I, too, am afraid but there is a limit to just how long one can live one's life always looking over the shoulder. Especially in these times when the need to be different, creative, becomes more and more urgent (because the traditional methods are not doing us any good anymore!), it behoves us to try and push the boundaries as far as we can. Too much **lip service** has been paid and it is time to sit up and take a good, honest hard look at ourselves. I count honesty and the courage to be open and admit shortcomings among the greatest of human virtues. Creativity must be allowed to flourish, not because it is going to be our final salvation (just think of what this new disease SARS has done/is doing even as this book goes to print) but because it has been the key factor differentiating us from all the other orders of creation. Many of us will recall the old lament:

Why must we only toil
we the roof and crown of things?

Found in Tennyson's poem *The Lotus Eaters*, this is to be understood in conjunction with the advice found in his other well-known poem, *Ulysses*:

Follow Knowledge like a sinking star
to the utmost bound of human thought.

Yes, this is what creativity is ultimately all about – going beyond belief, beyond expectations, beyond that utmost bound of human thought. Note **thought**, not just deed or action. Because the time is fast upon us when we might all be telepaths and will need to go beyond thought!

APPENDIX I

How Creative Am I?

If we are to launch onto a creativity path it might be useful to ask just how creative we are. Not because if we are found to be **uncreative** we give up, but knowing where we stand on the creativity chart might help us understand better the kinds of tools we will need to become effectively creative. **The Kirpal Inventory**™, is a short, simple and easy-to-do questionnaire which I have developed with the help of friends and colleagues. It teases us and at the same time places us on a continuum of **creativity-inclined.**

For each of the following statements, answer **Yes** or **No**. Honesty, of course, is of the essence!

1. I was born when the sky was bright with a silver lining.
2. My parents leapt with joy when they heard my first howl.
3. I always want to do things differently.
4. The other day I met an old man who asked me the way home. I told him he should try taking an aeroplane.
5. I usually tend to agree with my parents.
6. Most often I argue with those around me.
7. When I am given a lemon I want to make lemonade.
8. I like reading poems.
9. I think most people need plenty of sleep.
10. Whenever I am told to do something, I give it my unique touch.
11. If I am asked to choose between an apple and a durian I choose a durian.
12. When I play Scrabble® I always try and use the word **mo**.
13. I was invited to a costume party for Halloween; I dressed myself in masking tape.

14. Every time I see a poster advertising Coca-Cola, I want to change it into a Pepsi advertisement.

15. I am willing to kiss five frogs before finally kissing the prince.

16. Whenever I am told to do something I always ask myself **why**.

17. At a bus stop I saw a young girl trying to open her umbrella: I took the umbrella and with one flick got it opened.

18. I never use a pencil when I can use a pen.

19. I know that **coup de text** is a very good phrase to use.

20. I remember that when I was in Grade 5 of my elementary school I used to sleep during maths classes.

21. The other day I tried to make my watch talk to me about sex.

22. I think **love** means being able to say no.

23. Too much eating is good for the doctors.

24. If I made a new car I'd call it **mecar**.

25. I have often thought of marrying a mosquito.

26. I was asked by my teacher to write a sentence containing the words **man, woman, good**: I wrote, "**Good man wants good woman**".

27. I am by nature a follower of new ideas.

28. When my friend asked me to help him with some money, I worked out a repayment scheme so as to get my money back on time.

29. Whenever I am alone in a lift I imagine there are others with me.

30. If I am asked whether I am a **creative** person, I always answer **yes**.

31. Whenever I have to multiply 5 by 24 I usually do this by multiplying 5 by 12 and adding the sum.

32. I always smile at the person(s) who are in a lift with me.

33. If someone nods when I ask a question I assume he or she is agreeing with me.

34. I have frequently dreamt of inventing wing-like things so each of us can fly anytime we like.

35. Leadership is not a technique to be learnt but a relationship to be cultivated.

36. I cry every time I get my dreams mixed-up with my nightmares.

37. I don't believe that women should wear trousers.

38. I feel that cloning is the greatest bio-technological feat ever!

39. When I see a child dirty his or her fingers in mud I feel good because the child is exploring dirt.

40. I woke up to find the sky dull. I knew it was going to rain. I felt very happy.

41. They say creative people are easily provoked: I agree.

42. They say creative people are troublemakers: I agree.

43. They say creative people disturb stability: I agree.

44. They say creative people are subversive: I disagree.

45. I was a child when I made my first toy. I am still a child.

46. It is crazy to imagine that one day all humans will be able to walk through walls.

47. If someone called me a **dirty, low-life creep with nothing to recommend but handsome handouts of inflated ego**, I'd be flattered.

48. I simply love to dance.

49. Democracy is about people having a say in all that concerns them.

50. Creativity is about people knowing they are special.

On a rough scale (and it has to stressed that this is a rough guide) of 1-50, if you scored **Yes** more than 40 times, then you are well on the way to being a creative individual. Of course most of the statements can be subtly analyzed and both a **Yes** or **No** response could be **correct**. However, we are not concerned here so much about **rightness** or **wrongness** as we are with **attitude**. Creative people, it has been found over many years and in many different places, tend to have an **attitude** which is markedly different from – even opposite to – the common attitudes of most people. Creative people want to let others know they are different, that they think differently, feel differently and have different ideas. Creativity begins, we dare say, with having this special **attitude**. However, if you scored for instance 50 **No** or 50 **Yes** responses it would be hard to say you are creative because most creative people while being a little **extreme** don't usually recognize themselves as being **thoroughly** extreme! Scoring more than 45 **Yes** response is also going to prove worrisome because creative people tend to apply their left brain often when answering or responding to questions and many of the questions/statements just do not comfortably invite so many **Yes** responses! On the whole, though, the more **Yes** responses you have, the more **creativity inclined** you are. These statements have been carefully formulated, with in-built nuances suggesting possibilities of creative potential as evidenced by both historical and contemporary manifestations of the creative mode.

Scores: Yes

50–50 problematic (i.e., you could be **creativity inclined** but there are real problems preventing your **creativity** from manifesting itself positively)

38–44 **very** creativity inclined – you can (and do) achieve results

30–37 **quite** creativity inclined – you can (and ought to) do better

22–29 **moderately** creativity inclined – try and attend courses on **creativity/innovation** and see how your own creative tendencies can be put to good/better use

15–21 **not-so** creativity inclined – you have thought about creativity but it is not of any real interest/use to you (or your present preoccupation)

8–14 **hardly** creativity inclined – you have little or no use for anything associated with creativity on a personal basis

0–7 **problematic** – you could be **very** creativity inclined but tend to be dismissive/indifferent to the whole area of such discourse

APPENDIX II

Judging Creativity

Here is another illustration of how **creativity** works. I teach a course called Creative Thinking at the university. One day I came into the class, divided all my students into three groups (A, B, C) and told them to do something creative for the next 45 minutes and then return to class and share their creative experience. Groups A and C went away while Group B lingered. After a few minutes, Group B said, "Kirpal, can you tell us something to do?" I said, "Okay, why don't you guys get into a lift and go up and down 20 times and see what you experience." Group B went off.

After 45 minutes all three groups returned. Group A had gone out and sat around an old tree and talked with this tree. The group members each shared what the tree had told each of them. Group C went to the university canteen and came back with wonderful ideas as to how the different food stalls could better advertise themselves. Group B, of course, spoke about going up and down a lift 20 times.

Now, which of these three groups would you say was the most creative, second most creative and least creative? The answers, it seems to me, are obvious.

APPENDIX III

Exercise: Becoming Creative

Find a comfortable spot to sit. Having sat in this comfortable spot, shut your eyes and walk along a beach. You come across a shell which is begging you to throw it back into the water. You ask "Why?" and the shell says, "Because my family is there." Being a family person yourself you take pity on this shell and throw it back. After doing this you keep walking. Suddenly a cry is heard. You look around and there in the distance is someone trying to get your attention for help. You rush towards him. He turns out to be your brother, being attacked by a snake. You get a stick and beat the snake so that the snake slithers away. You turn around to talk to your brother. But he is not there. You are puzzled. You begin to wonder whether you were simply dreaming or whether your brother was really being attacked by a snake. As you walk along thinking about these matters, it occurs to you that you are merely engaged in an exercise using your imagination to release your creative self. You smile. You open your eyes and find that you have shifted in your sitting position.

This is a simple exercise and yet its experience is very complex. Creative people tend to have more **complex** experiences than their less-creative counterparts. Creative individuals tend to imagine a lot, dream a lot and as a result come up with fanciful, odd and even strange notions. Most people tend to be a little worried if they find that their siblings or good friends are creative.

Now think of a definite **creative** experience you have had and write it down here:

_____

_____

_____

_____

APPENDIX IV

Singapore Management University – A Bold Experiment

It is not usual for writers to focus on their own employers; well, at least, I am told, not in this culture here. But I have to be frank and honest because here is a specific instance which highlights both the great highs and the occasional lows of an organization wanting to be different and creative. I therefore seek the indulgence, in advance, of my superiors at the university if what I record here may sometimes prove just that little bit irksome.

Some years ago, especially with the feedback given by employers and visiting consultants as to the quality and type of graduates that Singapore needed for the new millennium, the government decided to launch a new university. Initially it was to be a kind of fusion with an existing organization, the Singapore Institute of Management, but, later the government decided that the new institution should be independent. A highly qualified team of professors and administrators was sought and the main goals and aims spelt out. I was invited to join the team in early 1999, and was among the very first to be rigorously interviewed by a team headed by the newly appointed President (Professor Janice Bellace from the esteemed Wharton School of Business, University of Pennsylvania) and given an appointment letter shortly after this. I formally joined the Singapore Management University (SMU) in February 2000.

It was the most exciting of places to be! Wow...here was a university like none I knew of – everything was to be different, from the admission process of students to the entire recruitment of staff. This was to be an American-oriented university, taking its cue chiefly from Wharton and also from other top universities. The aim was to ensure that a top-level university education would be made possible through special procedures affecting all levels of university functioning. Transparency was aimed for and those of us who recall, remember vividly some animated early discussions held with the president herself chairing the discussions and, frequently, deferring, to academic requests and views. As Wordsworth would have said:

It was a bliss to be alive then
But to be young was Heaven itself!

We were blissful and we were young. We still are, in the main. For me personally, the great excitement and challenge was being made coordinator of the new Creative Thinking Programme; the first I knew of (and still know of) anywhere in Asia, certainly the first in Singapore. Creative thinking (CT) as a subject was to be part of the **university-core**, every student entering SMU had to do CT and pass it. For me, this was a big challenge and a source of tremendous stimulation. Very rarely before had I ever, within the Singaporean context, been given such space, such a spur. At both my previous universities (the National University of Singapore and then the National Institute of Education of the Nanyang Technological University) the **pace** was mostly set and one did best by just doing what had always been done and following the leader's bidding. As the reader of this book will by now have found out, I did move away from the norm and frequently got taken to task for this. Ironically, many of the things I seem to have "fought" for are now very much in place, years after I had made the initial suggestions. So, is creativity always a matter of **timing**? Or of having good bosses, enlightened bosses who take things in tow and encourage creativity, new possibilities?

For too long the university education system had been almost totally dependent on impulse from our ex-colonial master, England, and the political leaders had now decided that the time had finally come for the critical shift to be made. So from a UK-type system, we at SMU were going to adopt the US system. And in the process we were tasked to go for the best, expenses notwithstanding. Not only has SMU become probably the first university in the world whose final architectural design was openly and publicly voted for by anyone visiting an open exhibition of the shortlisted designs held in 2001, but within the Singaporean context it has triumphed in open public debate and discussion conducted through endless columns and letters to the press, in demonstrating just how **different** it is. Make a difference, we were told, and so far we seem to have done excellently in this respect.

But my purpose of appending a discussion on and about SMU here is more specific: I want to outline, in brief, just how my own programme, the Creative Thinking course, has gone through changes in the three years that I have now taught it. It must be observed that each and every single student entering SMU has to be interviewed, either face-to-face or via telephone (if he or she comes from a country outside Singapore and cannot be physically present for the interview). We started by having each potential student interviewed by two professors; now, at least in the School of Business, we are starting to interview potential students en bloc, so we have about 10–20 students all seated together around 3–4 faculty and engaged in discussions. I personally believe that nothing, nothing can really replace the original plan: a 2-on-1 interview and I have stated openly that that first cohort of students we took in still seems to me to be the best ever. And I will attribute much of this to the admission criteria and process. (Readers might be interested to know that at SMU four criteria apply: the A-level results, the SAT I scores, an on-the-spot essay exercise, and the interview. Such a combination almost guarantees that only the very good, only those we really want, get in.) However, as the interviewing process gets diluted and as the essay topics – for me another great initiative here – become more predictable (in its first year we had very challenging essay topics, none like those the in-coming students might have been used to coming from their junior colleges or the polytechnics), the uniqueness of our students might change. I am told that mostly the reasons why we are in a sense becoming more and more **normal** in our admission procedures is because of the huge costs incurred as the number of students grow. Yes, the whole operation is expensive, very expensive, but I stand firm that it is expense well spent. Especially if we are to take in students who are not just **exam-smart** (these enter the other two universities very easily) but **life-smart**; students who are bursting with creative energies waiting to express themselves.

We have been extremely lucky in the sense that the university is under the strict purview of a board of trustees chaired by one of Singapore's top entrepreneurs and creative businessmen: Ho Kwon Ping, together with his dynamic wife, Claire Chiang, of the well-known Banyan Tree Resorts chain of luxury hotels. Given his own experiences, KP (as he is fondly called) has been open and flexible, and this has propelled SMU's journey. The university is also very fortunate in that it has a fairly free hand in most matters connected with university education and its status as a private university (private but publicly funded) allows it much leeway in dealing with sudden and awkward situations. From the very start it adopted a consultative approach in most aspects of university administration and policy and though the rules and guidelines keep changing as new situations arise or develop, the basic framework is, more or less, in place. Starting with just one school in 2000 (School of Business) it now has three other schools and may well establish two to three more in the coming years. Its faculty comes from around the world and its students, too. Among its creative initiatives is the requirement that all our students be attached for practical experience; we have the possibility of independent study negotiated between students and professors at the undergraduate level (most universities have this only at graduate level); we have compulsory community service – every student has to do about 80 hours of volunteer work to fulfil requirements for graduation. Students are encouraged to start their own activities, organize their own events and, generally, take ownership of their decisions and actions. I will not go into detail here of all the wonderful things SMU is becoming known for and for its educational vision of an open university of the future. Anyone interested should visit the website *www.smu.edu.sg.*

All of the above makes for an innovative, exciting, stimulating and, generally, vibrant creative university culture. However, as organizations grow, certain guidelines suddenly become policies and rules become harder to change and longer to negotiate. SMU has recently chartered its own Senate, a body which will assist the President and Senior Management in running the university so as to achieve and realize the best standards possible. As the charming Provost, Professor Tan Chin Tiong (himself a well-known marketing scholar), put to me: it is inevitable that as organizations grow, certain things "**become more onerous. It is easy to manage a few, much harder to manage masses**." So the question pops up: is it endemic with large organizations that creativity stands a lesser chance of real success? Is this the reason why the great universities of the world, MIT, Harvard, Stanford, Oxford, Cambridge, remain small in comparison to the huge institutions which graduate students as one would a regimental army? What is the link between size and creativity? This is a crucial question and one which needs to be answered by every individual and group keen on scoring success in creativity and innovative circles. We are told more than once that among the most creative organizations in the world are those like 3M: does such knowledge affect the way we ourselves see the relationship between size and creativity?

The Australian academic and writer, Syd Harrex, tells me that creativity can be taken to mean:

> A way of looking at life, things, ideas that conjure a new realization, a "shock of recognition" (Henry James' phrase in *The Ambassadors*); an original way of drawing attention to what was always known but now is apprehension comprehended as if for the first time; and vice versa, of course. Defamiliarizing the familiar so that in one of Shakespeare's many post-modern mirrors you discover "a local habitation and a name". But beware of retina damage – or worse, macular degeneration – when your eye is rolling in too fine a frenzy.

Now, the complex literary allusions notwithstanding (and I must warn the reader that Syd is a voracious reader himself and has a prodigious intellect so that very often only he truly realizes the depth and subtlety of his wit!), what is being communicated here is, surely, the sense of the **new**, the sense that, wow! Here is a remarkably new and fresh way of looking at things and doing things and seeing things, much like Groucho Marx when he said, "**If you want to watch a comic strip, see me in the shower.**" Most people are either irritated by such wit or put off by it, but, say whatever you like, there is creativity here. Rolling in too fine a frenzy can be taken to mean that there could be dangers in being overly creative, emotions can be hurt and personalities unnecessarily wounded or harmed. I agree. I have seen very gifted individuals come to no good because they got on the wrong side of life, forgot they have to live and work with others and allowed their own sense of their creative genius to infect their entire existence with the net result that they found themselves totally alone, isolated. Usually, such people exit quite dramatically, or just withdraw into some kind of oblivion. Creativity is so easy to kill, destroy, set aside. I know because I see this happening daily. And it is sad and painful to watch people with good, fresh ideas being cast aside because they don't fit into the mould. So being creative is much, much more than simply knowing you can do things differently or more excitingly than others; it is also knowing that the world around you may not think you are creative or imagine you, of all people, can come up with exciting new ideas. Creative people have to learn some good interpersonal skills and know when, as one of my former bosses used to say, to shut up. The pity is that frequently creative people shut up and remain that way forever afterwards.

Young creative people need inspiration and hence at SMU we try and inspire our charges in all ways we can. Anyone who knows Singapore and walks into our campus will know immediately just how different we are. The signs of our students' creativity are everywhere and we try and ensure that they do not tire of attempting to be different, to be creative. But incentives and motivating factors can and do have limits and I am sure the university will not be in a position to provide the same kind of creative ethos once it grows outwards and moves to embrace the same kind of benchmarks as other universities. This is the dilemma facing us: if we are going to set our standards by the so-called benchmarking ritual, then we may lose out to those who specialize in doing this sort of a thing and working to get their target goals achieved. Creativity cannot – and should not – do this. Creativity will move on its own steam with its own direction and without always worrying about what others say or think. My students always ask me, so is there an overriding subjective assessment invariably present in every creative exercise, event and test? Yes, I say, but when we really check it out it is surprising just how often we tend to agree and see that which is creative as creative! My students agree with me on this.

I give my students all manner of tasks to do. Here is a sample of an exercise done on **My Ideal Classroom**.

> The cubic classroom is modified into a spherical room and run by a special program. So the whole classroom is computerized. All the walls are made by TV screens. In the centre of the sphere, there is a spinning disc which can rotate 360 degree and that is where we sit as well as stand. Of course, you won't fall to the

ground when you are in the position, upside down due to the centripetal force which will glue you onto the disc.

Welcome boarding our ideal classroom, please make yourself comfortable.

Before the class starts, you will be left with these blank TV screens for one hour so that your mind and body can cool down. And you should enter into the stage that nothing in your mind. You only breathe in and out.

Now, you will see eight pictures on the screen. They include sun, rainbow, forest, stones, fresh fruits, animals, children and last but not the least a picture of 26 letters and numbers from 0 to 9. These are chosen because they are the essential elements in our living world. Notice that each picture is actually composed by identical small squares. These squares can be shifted around from one end of the sphere to the end so that you can actually rearrange them in the way you like. The shift here is in fact that you touch both the original and designated parts on the screen so that computer will help swap them automatically. Imagine if each picture is cut into 64 pieces, you will have 512 pieces altogether. How many combinations you can get from these 512 pieces? Moreover, the graphics on each piece is changeable in terms of color and shape. So the sun can be green in color and trapezium in shape.

So far maybe you think this doesn't help to stimulate your ideas at all. And it is not much different from what you watch in the show. Let me tell you the most wonderful part of spherical classroom.

Remember the spinning disc? That is the magic part.

Having various pictures or art works, what can you see from them? Start the engine of our spinning disc. At various speed, you will catch different parts of pictures in your mind, and we you gather them together and form them into a new picture, you actually come out something totally new and different. How about having some rotations? What will you see if you are upside down? A rainbow becomes a boat? Or you could be more imaginative. Just let your thoughts flow like the running stream.

Do you like it?

That is my room.

Well? This is the vision of a student from China: Zhou Bing, one of the more actively creative students I've had this past year.

As you can gather from her composition, Zhou Bing has an imaginative mind and she is not afraid to let the wild ideas take root and articulate themselves. I found, a little to my dismay, that the Singaporean students attempting the same individual assignment seemed not to be as daringly imaginative as Zhou Bing. So I asked her how she came up with the ideas. "I just sat down under the trees one day and thought to myself, 'Girl, you have the best chance to design and shape your own learning environment,' and I came up with this." Good. I wish more students will do this sitting under trees and come up with wild ideas. We don't have enough of them, even here at SMU. We need more.

Here is another example of a creative-thinking assignment: a poem, written in response to the theme **How The Waters Moved Me**.

How the waters move me
Doctors think
Blood cleanses
Urine purges
Saliva stimulates
Tears humanifies
But great monsters intoxicate
Nature Lovers proclaim
Fountains intrigue
Sea calms
Rain revitalizes
But great monsters flood
I say
Snow
Stranger's smile
Folding a paper crane
Licking the last bit of home-baked Tiramisu
Are
    All
      Moving
        Streams
          Of
           Lingering
             Moments
   Enriching
   My Life

When I first saw what Amy Fong, the student who devised that, had done, I wondered whether she knew what in fact was going on! I thought it was some kind of computer glitch! But no, she assured me, this was intended. The waters did **move** her as is evident from the movement of the poem's letters and words. A different kind of creativity at work here, transcending the normal idea of just penning a rhyme. Did I think this was a very good effort? Well, yes and no. Yes, because it **is** novel, and no, because it is not really a poem which says anything too profound. But, I ask myself, is this my problem because I happen to come from a broad-based literary background or is it true that this is not that great a poem though it is engaging in its own way and so the narrative(s) here could continue ad infinitum. The point is our students at SMU are exposed to creativity at a very **raw** level and from here they develop their own unique brand and image. It is, of course, my hope that these students will employ what they have picked up through the different experiences in the CT classes/sessions (we do plenty of non-verbal exercises to stimulate the right brain!) in all their other subjects.

I want to end this brief description of SMU's efforts at making our students more creative, or at least more intelligently and sensitively aware of their own creativity, by showing you just some of the many wonderful pieces of creative work my students have done, crafted and created in the three years since we started. By all looks creative thinking **is** driving the energies of these young men and women and it looks as if there is no stopping them. Thanks to the vision of the founding faculty of SMU, our students do and are going to have that little **edge** over many others because here we do make creativity a real priority.

A Day in the Life of a SMU Student

Try and figure out what the typical SMU day consists of. Five different activities are depicted.

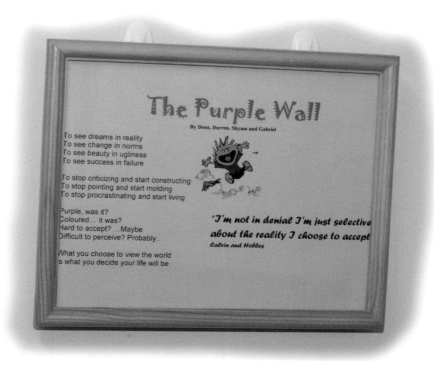

The Purple Wall

By Dous, Darren, Shyam and Gabriel

To see dreams in reality
To see change in norms
To see beauty in ugliness
To see success in failure

To stop criticizing and start constructing
To stop pointing and start molding
To stop procrastinating and start living

Purple, was it?
Coloured... it was?
Hard to accept? ...Maybe
Difficult to perceive? Probably..

What you choose to view the world
Is what you decide your life will be

"I'm not in denial I'm just selective about the reality I choose to accept
Calvin and Hobbes

This was a "mystery" thing ... I didn't know what the students were up to. One morning I came to my office and saw the entire wall on the side covered with newspapers. The Deputy Dean of Business kindly consented to say a few words about creativity and its inspirational as well as dynamic modalities. When he declared the wall "open", wow, this was what emerged. The group that did the project talked about perception and perspective being essentially individual things and said that if we clue ourselves sufficiently, the white wall could become a purple wall. What do you, my dear reader, think?

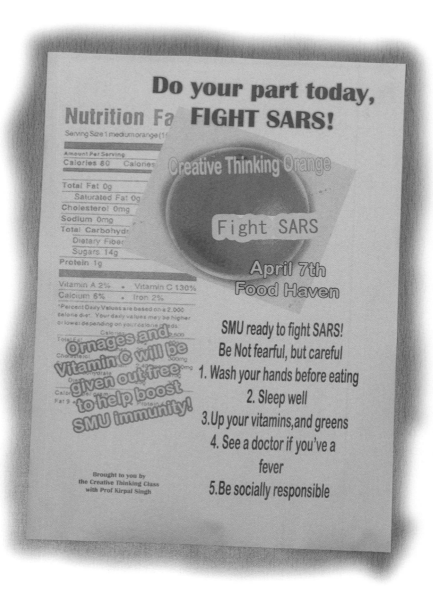

The SARS battle – one of my Creative Thinking students decided to be proactive and do something about the SARS campaign on campus. This was the poster-sheet she pasted on every faculty's door. I thought this was interesting and displayed a certain degree of proactive-innovative action in times of crises.

This picture containing nine squares is a teaser. You are to try and find the letters SMU in all nine squares. Most people seem to get about seven correct. What about you?

The tradition of mask-making is rich and has a long and respected history. One of my groups made these masks and demonstrated their very different uses through actual playacting.

Entrepreneurship in the era of Globalisation 24th Sep.

This page is in black and white

SIF-ASEAN Student Fellowship & SMU Ventures

... *Unfortunately, life seldom is.*

It is good to know that our SMU students are starting to display some level of wit (sometimes tinged with humour, often not!) in their handouts/brochures. This was the programme sheet for a recent seminar on globalization and entrepreneurship.

I thought long and hard about showing this, and finally decided, why not? My office is a huge, creative mess, with student projects lying everywhere. Thanks to Charlie (who hails from Madang in Papua New Guinea), order is preserved in the midst of apparent chaos. I must confess that I find my own office a very inspiring and creative space. Here is where I conceive most of my ideas and the first words, say, of a new poem or story.

APPENDIX V

Creativity in the Arts, Science and Technology

This paper was given some two years ago. I remember that it made some listeners sit up and think. Indeed many emailed me to say just how important it was that someone like me took it upon myself to say, in public, what really needed to be said. So I stick my turban out. People tell me that not much has changed since I gave this speech. They tell me, "Please say it again." So, here it is again, for public record and for permanence, too.

Public Forum
24 November 2001
National University of Singapore

I want to begin by asking a few simple questions: how do we recognize **creativity**? How do we recognize a **creative** person? What, in the end, does the word **creativity** itself mean?

No one gathered here today will be naive enough to offer simple answers or responses to these questions because people have debated and discussed them for centuries. And yet, and yet, for all their complexity, these questions also signal something we all seem to know or understand. In other words, no matter how we define the words, we know creativity when we experience it and we recognize a creative person when we come across one. However, different cultures reward this **recognition** very differently and this, it seems to me, is the more fundamental question: are we in Singapore ready to reward the recognition of the creative individual and the recognition of creativity?

Today's forum clearly suggests that we are. In recent years there has been much talk and discussion about **creativity**; courses on the subject are legion and everyone seems to be engaged in one way or another in fostering creative conduct. Creativity has become, suddenly, a buzzword. Bees buzz and where there is a gathering of bees there is bound to be honey! Honey, I am told on good authority, attracts birds and this is how we get the interesting formulation of the birds and the bees which, of course, when put in conjunction, can lead to huge levels of productivity!

Seriously, though, we also hear people saying **no money, no honey, baby**! What this means exactly I am not sure, but what I do know – and this is going to be the burden of my presentation – is that money alone, even though it might give us a lot of honey, will never make for creativity. It is, I believe, a lesson we in Singapore will have to learn and it appears we are learning it in an expensive and costly manner. Whenever we want to focus on the creative and creativity, the first thing which most people tend to come up with is: give me money, give us the funds, facilitate and provide us with this, that and the other.

I want to state here that even if we provided all the money, gave all the funds, made this, that and the other available, there is no guarantee that we will become creative.

To my mind, **nurturing creativity and the creative individual requires a total revolution, nothing short of a complete and absolute change in the way we think, the way we behave, the way we judge**. Yes, especially the last item on which most of us seem to have a ready judgement. The nature of creativity is that it defies **judgement** precisely because it is new, different and original. Are we truly ready for this revolution? Are we ready to accept that the creative person is bound to prove upsetting, disturbing and even troublesome precisely because he or she brings to us a new and completely different way of looking at things? Of doing things? Of behaving? I think most of us are not ready because we are threatened by creativity and creative people. We feel small; we feel a loss of face; we feel that to acknowledge creativity is to admit that we ourselves are somehow below expectation, that others are better than us. This is a peculiar disease particularly relevant to many who occupy middle to upper-middle positions in our numerous bureaucracies. I recall one of our ministers commenting that part of the problem for us in Singapore today is that the head is very mobile and active, but from the neck downwards there is a block! So creativity chokes.

I want to outline four areas of crucial significance if we are to move forward in our quest for creativity:

1. Fun

For some odd reason we in Singapore tend to associate fun with funny and therefore tend not to respect anyone who has fun doing what he or she is doing. I am putting things mildly. I know from bitter personal experience that respect here seems to be linked very closely to being serious; that is, if you crack jokes and laugh, you are bound not to be taken seriously even if you have serious things to say and share. I am afraid creativity must have room for fun and even the funny. Because when you are creative you live, and when you live with a passion you enjoy living, and you enjoy life therefore you have fun! Let me illustrate: I often begin classes in creative thinking by asking my students to reflect on lines such as **Jack and Jill went up the hill/To fetch a pail of water** or **My love's like a red, red rose**. Why, I ask my students did Jack and Jill have to go **up** to fetch water? And why does good old Robbie Burns say love's like a **red** rose? (Will a green rose or a pink rose or a yellow rose **not** be love?) My students invariably laugh. Good. I tell jokes to make a point. For example there is a story about how Malaysia's Vision 2020 came about. Dr M and colleagues visited a *kampung*. On every rooftop they observed a TV aerial but each house they entered seemed not to have a TV set. Dr M could not help, in frustration, asking the *penghulu* of the *kampung* why there were TV aerials but no TV sets. Apparently this is what the *kampung* headman told the prime minister: "*Itu lah, yang hal susah. Kita ni ada tali, tapi tak ada vision.*" (That is the problem. We here have the aerial but no vision.) Dr M immediately saw the problem and came up with Vision 2020! Creativity allows plenty of room for making jokes thus allowing very important but highly sensitive issues to be raised and valued without hurt and pain.

Where is Singapore's Lat or Colette? Let our bright and beautiful young minds in schools draw cartoons instead of carrying huge worksheets home every day! Let our students play games and experience life with a passion instead of burdening them with threats of elimination if they do not score good grades in every test or exam. Let us re-examine this entire exam-bogged mentality of us Singaporeans to find out honestly where, after all these years, our super examination-achievers have got us. I once told the late Dr Tay Eng Soon that going by the number of As our students get at the O-level and A-level examinations we ought to have at least 20 Nobel Prize winners by now, especially in the field of the sciences! Sorry, these are touchy, very sensitive topics but all our nerves have to be tickled in order that they might function in a creative manner.

2. Fear

We can only have fun if we have no fear. Honesty must compel us to admit that far too many of us still live and work in fear: fear of reprimand, fear of doing the wrong thing, especially fear of failure. Yes, we hear a lot about getting rid of fear and not being afraid to make mistakes; we are exhorted to take risks but who, truly, is going to take risks when failure seems to be quite severely punished? Schools, for example, that do not stress too much high examination grades but encourage a rich environment of creative space get fewer rewards; this is indirect punishment. Many who go out and try a new way of doing things but don't bring back the goodies are warned or sometimes simply sacked! Students who say, compose beautiful songs but don't score high marks in certain subjects deemed crucial, end up roaming the streets because they could not make it at the higher levels of scholarship. Bosses fear subordinates who speak their minds; subordinates fear bosses who have tunnel vision and operate from a seat of terrible insecurity. I have experienced both. It is my fervent hope that as we move along this wonderful new century, we have the courage and wisdom to see beauty in the many creative people around us as well as the generosity to reward creativity richly. My friends tell me that to be **original** is often to invite elimination. For example, if I told my boss that instead of coming to work at 9 a.m. every day I'd come at 11 a.m. and go home at 8 p.m., chances are that I am not going to get very far because without even asking for the wisdom of my workplan my boss is going to say, "**Sure, go work for yourself!**" Far too frequently those in power dismiss new ideas as being silly, unworkable, costly, useless, without even listening to them or giving the individuals behind these new ideas the chance to prove, demonstrate their workability and worth. It takes a strong, confident personality to stake a claim for creativity and it requires a strong, confident personality to recognize and reward such a claim. Both are in short supply in Singapore.

3. Freedom

Creativity thrives in a free environment. Freedom here does not mean breaching codes of public conduct or morality. No, it means the ability to try out new ways of thinking, working and even behaving. Let me give you two specific examples. In one school teachers got together and requested their principal's permission to wear bright, colourful clothes instead of the usual drab (but official-looking) ones. They convinced their principal that even though initially some parents and fellow teachers from other schools might not think them worthy of the label **teacher**, in the longer term everyone would be happier because their colourful clothes would bring colourful disposition and happy people learn faster. The principal was sympathetic and willingly gave the teachers the go-ahead. The school's overall morale shot up as did collegiality, and even end-of-year examination performances! Now some of you might say this is not being creative as such, merely wanting change, but **creativity begins with wanting change**. My second example comes from the US. In 1997 I was invited as Distinguished International Writer by the world-famous Iowa International Writing Programme. The Director of the programme then, Professor Clark Blaise, a well-known Canadian writer, astonished me with the story of getting his first bank loan. Being young and having just arrived in Iowa, Clark told me, meant setting up house, etc. He needed money to buy a house and other things. The only security he had was his small salary. He met the bank manager and the meeting concluded with the bank manager saying he was sorry he couldn't help Clark with a higher loan amount because the bank demanded some form of security. In exasperation, Clark told the bank manager that the only thing he had which he could offer as security was the newly completed manuscript of his novel. Clark was then not so well-known as a writer. Guess what? The bank manager said, "You're on, buddy!" And Clark Blaise got his money. Imagine how many Singaporean bank managers would have the freedom (and if they have the freedom will use this freedom) to make such decisions? Many, I fear, will think of this as a joke!

Freedom means giving creativity a real chance to prove itself without silly restrictions or restrictions which are fast being realized to be blocks to creativity. For instance, you give a staff member a beautiful office but then say, you can't paint the walls because it will upset the overall aesthetics! Or you give a scientist a laboratory but say he or she can only use it between seven in the morning and midnight! I was in the world-famous MIT recently and the professors there work 24 hours a day and almost everything functions 24 hours a day. If we want creativity, let's follow the examples of the best and not get bogged down by petty parameters of boundaries which worked in a previous millennium but which can only hinder our efforts at becoming a creative nation.

4. Trust

My last point is also my most important one because this is what I think we need most if we are to prosper as a creative nation: trust. We don't trust each other very much. The culture of trust seems to be almost wholly new to most in Singapore. Trust is tied up with the larger issue of **accountability**. I agree that this is a difficult area to negotiate but negotiate it we must; otherwise, as more than one foreign creative person has told me (and not only me as many others here might bear witness), we will never become truly creative. Trust means letting people go; trust means not fussing overmuch about slight variations in itemized programmes or budgeted items. For instance, we are all encouraged these days to apply for funds to do creative projects. Let's say we apply and get the funds. At Point X we asked for, let's say, $10,000 to go to the UK and another $6,000 to employ a research assistant. Come Point Z and we realize that, really, we should visit Canada (and not the UK) and that instead of a research assistant we need funds to watch 50 films connected with our creative project. Will we be reprimanded? Why did you not do your homework properly before submitting your budget for the research grant? Why were you so careless? Why did you change your mind? Why should we pay you to just watch films? And so on and so forth. If this is the mindset of those who approve or give us funds, then I am sorry to say we will again not go very far for the frustration will kill all joy of the creative project and dampen the spirit so much that instead of having an energized, happy person working on the project you will get an angry, upset and dismayed body spending more time and energy filling forms and justifying changes than actually working on the creative project. My belief is that we should trust those we finance more; sure, accountability must be there, but it must not be a hindrance or a deterrence; it should genuinely seek to enhance the work on the creative project and not get buried in a pile of paperwork; those who sit in judgment here must have the courage to allow for flexibility in the use of research and project funds for creativity works in strange, usually unpredictable ways. I was told by Dr Stephen Hazell, Head of Drama at the National Institute of Education, that a friend of his was given a one-year grant to go to Stanford and do nothing but **think**. Now **that** is trust. Imagine – would bosses here give us money for a whole year to do nothing but think? I recall a conversation with the head of Bell Laboratories in which he is supposed to have said that they fund around 100 scientists and even if only one or two of these scientists produced something truly creative, they'd be very, very happy. In other words, creativity does not come cheap, either in terms of money or in terms of effort and energy. It takes a lot to trust people but trust we must. If it is risky, well, let's put our mouth where our money is and say, good, we trust you to do your best. That's the most we can reasonably ask of our people. And let us not be too quick to judge and lose our trust in them for creative individuals are a precious possession and if we don't honour them they will go elsewhere (as many have done).

So the point is initiative and innovative thinking must be encouraged and rewarded. There are stories galore of huge corporations mistaking creativity for silliness and paying a very heavy price to get the silly people back! (3M is one such corporation.) We live in very challenging times and our prime minister has given us a fantastic theme for use: **Learning Schools, Thinking Nation**. It behoves us to be kind and gentle towards those who are trying their desperate best to contribute meaningfully to the healthy development of creativity in Singapore whether this be in the arts, the sciences or in technological inventions. Please allow me to end by reminding ourselves that even God in His eternal wisdom advised: *He only helps those who help themselves.* So God rewards the proactive, those who take the initiative and move.

Movers and shakers do more than just move or shake – they bring about fundamental changes in the ways in which we relate to the world and to ourselves. Let us recognize and reward amply and ably - and before it is too late - those who help us realize and understand what being creative means!

Thank you.

ABOUT THE AUTHOR

Dr Kirpal Singh is fast emerging as one of the most powerful voices in the international arena of creativity. A keenly sought-after speaker at important international forums, seminars and workshops on creativity/ innovation, Dr Singh has given several critically acclaimed keynote speeches in many countries about the relationship between cultures, languages and creativity. Prior to joining the newly established Singapore Management University where he facilitates the core university module of Creative Thinking, Dr Singh taught at the National University of Singapore and the National Institute of Education. In all 3 institutions Dr Singh worked tirelessly to try to bring about fundamental changes to existing mindsets. Dr Singh has also taught and researched in several universities around the world and is well-known for publishing articles and books which challenge existing assumptions, norms and standards. As a fictionist and poet, Dr Singh has been invited to the world's major Writers Festivals (Edinburgh, Toronto, York, Cambridge, Adelaide) and in 1997, was Distinguished International Writer at the world-famous Iowa International Writing Program. Many of his creative works have been dramatised, choreographed and set to music.